THE PERFECT WAY

T0126337

OSHO

"Do not tarry anymore,
One has but four days.
Two go in desiring, two in waiting."

Extemporaneous talks given by Osho
in Ranakpur, Rajasthan, India

the
perfect way

OSHO

Originally published in Hindi as *Sadhana Path*. The material in this book is
from a series of talks by Osho. The complete OSHO text archive can be
found via the online OSHO Library at www.osho.com

OSHO and OSHO Vision are registered trademarks of OSHO
International Foundation www.osho.com/trademarks

OSHO MEDIA INTERNATIONAL
New York – Zurich – Mumbai
an imprint of
OSHO INTERNATIONAL
www.osho.com/oshointernational

Distributed by Publishers Group Worldwide
www.pgw.com

Library of Congress Catalog-In-Publication Data is available

Printed in USA by Bang Printing

ISBN: 978-1-938755-98-9
This title is also available in eBook format ISBN: 978-0-88050-611-3

CONTENTS

CHAPTER 1

Prologue: Invitation Into Light

I see man engulfed in a deep darkness. He has become like a house where the lamp has gone out on a dark night. Something in him has been extinguished. But that which has been extinguished can be relit.

I see as well that man has lost all direction. He has become like a boat that has lost its way on the high seas. He has forgotten where he is to go and what he is to be. But the memory of what has been forgotten can be reawakened in him.

Hence, although there is darkness there is no reason for despair. In fact, the deeper the darkness the closer the dawn. I see a spiritual regeneration for the whole world on the horizon. A new man is about to be born and we are passing through the throes of his birth. But this regeneration needs the cooperation of each one of us. It is to come through us, hence we cannot remain mere spectators. We must give way for this rebirth within ourselves.

The approach of that new day, of that dawn, is possible only if each one of us fills himself with light. It is in our hands to turn that possibility into an actuality. We all are the bricks of that palace of tomorrow and we all are the rays of light out of which the future sun will be born. We are the creators, not just spectators. It is not only a creation of the future, it is a creation of the present itself, it is the creation of ourselves. It is through creating himself that man creates humanity. The individual is the unit of the whole and it is through him that both evolution and revolution can take place. You are that unit.

This is why I want to call you. I want to awaken you from your slumber. Don't you see that your lives have become utterly meaningless and useless, totally boring? Life has lost all meaning and purpose. But this is natural. If there is no light in man's heart there cannot be any meaning in his life. There cannot be any bliss in man's life if there is no light in his inner being.

The fact that we find ourselves overburdened with meaninglessness today is not because life in itself is meaningless. Life is infinite meaningfulness, but we have forgotten the path that leads to that meaningfulness and fulfillment. We simply exist and have no contact with life. This is not living, it is just waiting for death. And how can waiting for death be anything but boring? How can it be bliss?

I have come here to tell you this very thing: there is a way to awaken from this bad dream that you have mistaken for life. The path has always been there. The path that leads from darkness to light is eternal. It is there for certain, but you have turned away from it. I want you to turn toward it. This path is dharma, religion. It is the means of rekindling the light in man; it gives direction to man's drifting boat. Mahavira has said that religion is the only island of safety, the anchor, the destination and the refuge for those being swept away by the rapid current of the world with its old age and its death.

Do you have a thirst for the light that fills life with bliss? Do you have a longing for the truth that unites man with immortality? If so, I invite you into that light, into that bliss, into that deathlessness. Please accept my invitation. It is simply a matter of opening your eyes, and you inhabit a new world of light. You don't have to do anything else, you only have to open your eyes. You just have to wake up and look.

Nothing in man can really be extinguished nor can he lose his direction, but if he keeps his eyes closed the darkness spreads everywhere and all sense of direction is lost. With closed eyes he is a beggar; with open eyes he is an emperor.

I am calling you to come out from your dream of being a beggar and wake up into your reality of being an emperor. I wish to transform your defeat into victory, I wish to transform your darkness into light, I wish to transform your death into deathlessness. Are you ready to embark upon this voyage with me?

CHAPTER 2

Listening with the Heart

Conscious soul,

First of all, please accept my love. It is the only thing with which I can welcome you in the loneliness and seclusion of these hills. In fact I have nothing else to give you. I want to share with you the infinite love that closeness with existence has created in me. I want to distribute it. And the wonder of it is that the more I share it, the more it grows! Perhaps real wealth is that which increases with distribution. The wealth that decreases by sharing is not real wealth at all. Will you then accept my love?

I see acceptance in your eyes and I see also that your eyes have become filled with love in response. Love invokes love and hate invokes hate. Whatever we give returns to us. This is an eternal law. So whatever you wish to receive is what you should give to the world. You cannot receive flowers in exchange for thorns.

I see flowers of love and peace blossoming in your eyes. I am deeply gratified by this. Now we are not many here: love joins together and turns the many into one. Physical bodies are separate and will continue to be separate, but there is something behind the bodies which meets in love, which becomes one in love. It is only after this unity, this oneness that something can be said and understood. Communication is only possible in love and in love alone.

We have gathered in this lonely place so that I can say something to you and you can listen to me. This saying and this listening is not possible without an undercurrent of love. The doors of the heart open only to love. And remember it is only when one hears with the heart and not with the head that listening happens. You may ask, "Does the heart hear as well?" I would say that whenever listening happens it is always through the heart. So far the head has never heard anything. The head is stone deaf. And this is also true of speaking. Only when words come from the heart are they meaningful. Only when words come from the heart do they have the fragrance of fresh flowers; otherwise they are not only stale and faded, they are artificial – plastic flowers.

I shall pour out my heart to you, and if your hearts let me in there will be meeting and communication. And then in that moment of meeting, that which words are incapable of expressing is also communicated. Many unsaid things are heard in this way – that which cannot be put into words, that which lies between the lines is also communicated. Words are very impotent indications, but if listened to in total peace of mind and in silence they become potent. This is what I call listening with the heart.

But as it is, even while listening to someone else we remain full of our own thoughts. That is "false hearing." Then you are not a *shravak*, a listener. You are only under the illusion that you are listening, but as a matter of fact you are not.

For "right hearing" it is necessary for the mind to be in a completely silent state of watchfulness. When you are only listening and not doing anything else, only then are you able to hear and understand, and that understanding becomes a light and a transformation within you. If it does not happen in this way, you are not listening to anyone but yourself – you remain surrounded by the tumult raging within you. And when you are engaged in such a way nothing can be communicated to you. Then you appear to be seeing but you are not; you appear to be listening but you are not.

Christ has said, "Those who have eyes to see, see. Those who have ears to hear, hear." Did those he was talking to not have eyes and ears? Of course they had eyes and ears, but the mere presence of eyes and ears is not enough for seeing and for hearing. Something more is needed and without it the existence or nonexistence of eyes and ears is the same. That something more is inner silence and watchful awareness. It is only when these qualities are there that the doors of the mind are open and something can be said and heard.

I expect this kind of hearing from you during the period of this meditation camp. Once you have learned it, it becomes your lifelong companion. It alone can rid you of trivial preoccupations. You can awaken to the great mysterious universe outside and you can experience the eternal, infinite light of consciousness hidden behind the tumult of the mind.

Right seeing and right hearing are not merely a necessity for this meditation camp but are the foundation of all right living. Just as everything is clearly reflected in a lake that is totally calm, without ripples, that which is the truth, that which is the divine will be reflected in you when you become calm and still like the lake.

I am seeing such silence arising in you. Your eyes – the thirst that I see coming to life in you – are inviting me to say what I wish to say. They are urging me to reveal the truths I have seen which have moved my soul; your hearts are eager and impatient to understand them. Seeing that you are so willing and ready, my heart is also getting ready to pour out to you. In these peaceful surroundings and with your peaceful state of mind, I will certainly be able to say what I wish to say to all of you. If I were to find deaf hearts in front of me, I would refrain. Doesn't the light remain outside when it finds the doors of your house closed? In the same way I often stand outside many houses. But it is a good sign that your doors are open. It is a good beginning.

From tomorrow morning we will begin our five-day sojourn of the meditation experiment. As a background to this, I would now like to say a few things to you. For meditation, for the realization of truth, the soil of our minds has to be prepared in the same way as one prepares the soil for the cultivation of flowers. So, I would like you to understand a few sutras, a few key points.

The first sutra is: Live in the present. During the camp days don't be carried away by your mechanical current of thinking about the past and the future. Because of that, the living moment, the moment that really exists, is wasted and it passes away uselessly. Neither the past nor the future exists. One is only in the memory, the other only in imagination. Only the present is the real and the living moment. And if the truth is to be known it can only be known through being in the present.

During these days of meditation, consciously keep yourselves free from the past and the future. Accept that they do not exist. Only the moment at hand, the moment you are in, exists. You have to live in it and to live it totally.

Tonight go to sleep as soundly as though your whole past has been dropped. Die to the past. And in the morning wake up as a new man in a new morning. Don't let the same one who went to bed get up. Let him go to sleep for good. Let the one who is ever new and ever fresh awake instead.

Keep this living in the present continuously in your remembrance around the clock, and keep aware so that mechanical thinking about the past and future does not start up. To remain watchful is enough for this. If you remain watchful, it cannot be triggered. Consciousness destroys the habit.

The second sutra is: Live naturally. Man's entire behavior is artificial and formal. We always keep ourselves wrapped in a phony cloak and because of this covering we gradually forget our own reality. You have to shed this false skin and throw it away. We have gathered here not to stage a drama but to know and to realize ourselves. Just as actors in a play remove their costumes and make up and put them aside after the performance, in these five days, you must remove your false masks and throw them away. Let that which is original and natural in you come out – and live in it. Meditation grows only in a simple and natural life.

During these days of meditation, know that you hold no position, you are not special, you have no status. Take away all these masks. You are simply you, an ordinary human being with no name, no status, no class, no family, no caste – just a nameless person, a very ordinary individual. You have to live like this. And remember this is also our actual reality.

The third sutra is: Live alone. A life of meditation takes birth in complete aloneness, when one is all alone. But generally man is never alone. He is always surrounded by others. And when he is not in a crowd outwardly, he is in a crowd inwardly. This crowd has to be dispersed.

Do not allow the crowd to gather within you. And on the outside also live by yourself as if you are all alone at this camp. You don't have to maintain relations with anyone else. In the midst of these countless relationships you have forgotten yourselves. All these relationships – that you are someone's enemy or friend, father or son, wife or husband – have so engulfed you that you are unable to know yourself in your own individuality.

Have you ever tried to imagine who you are, away from these relationships of yours? Have you ever discarded the garb of these relationships and seen yourself without them? Differentiate yourself from all these relationships and know that you are not the son of your father and mother, not the husband of your wife, not the father of your children, not the friend of your friends, not the enemy of your enemies – and what remains is your real being. That remaining entity is what you are in yourself. During these days you have to live alone in that being.

By following these sutras your mind will come to the state that is an absolute necessity for realizing peace and truth. Along with these three sutras, I wish to explain to you the two kinds of meditation we will begin to do from tomorrow morning.

The first meditation is for the morning. During this meditation you must hold your spine erect, close your eyes and keep your neck straight. Your lips should be closed and your tongue should touch the palate. Breathe slowly but deeply. Keep your attention near the navel. Remain aware of the tremor you feel at the navel because of the breathing. This is all you have to do. This experiment calms the mind and empties thoughts completely. From this emptiness one ultimately enters within oneself.

The second meditation is for the night. Spread your body on the floor comfortably and let all your limbs relax completely. Close your eyes and for about two minutes suggest to yourself that the body is relaxing. Gradually the body will become relaxed. Then for two minutes suggest that your breathing is becoming quiet and your breathing will become quiet. Finally, for another two minutes suggest that thoughts are coming to a halt. This determined suggestion leads to complete relaxation, tranquility and emptiness. When the mind has become perfectly calm, be totally awake in your inner being and be a witness to this peace. This witnessing will lead you to your self.

You must do these two meditations. As a matter of fact they are really artificial devices and you are not to get stuck to them. With their help, the mind's restlessness dissolves. And just as we no longer need a ladder after climbing, one day we will have to give up these devices as well.

Meditation attains perfection the day it becomes unnecessary. This very state is *samadhi*, enlightenment.

Now the night is well advanced and the sky is filled with stars. The trees and the valleys have gone to sleep. We will also go to sleep now. How quiet and silent it all is! We will also merge into this silence. In deep sleep, in dreamless sleep we go to the very place where the divine dwells. This is the spontaneous, nonconscious *samadhi* that nature has bestowed upon us. Through meditation we also reach the same place, but then we are conscious and aware. This is the only difference. And it is a great difference indeed. In the former we go to sleep, in the latter we become awakened.

Let us now go into sleep with the hope that going into awakening will also become possible. When hope is accompanied by determination and endeavor it certainly becomes fulfilled.

May existence guide us along the path. This is my only prayer.

CHAPTER 3

Thought Birth Control

Conscious soul,

I am delighted to see you. You have gathered in this solitary place in your search to attain godliness, to find the truth, to know your own self, your being. But may I ask you a question: Is what you are seeking separate from you? You can search for someone who is separate from you, but how can you seek that which you yourself are? Your own self cannot be sought in the way in which everything else is sought, because in this case there is no difference between the one who is seeking and the one who is being sought. You can seek out the world but you cannot seek out your self. He who goes out in search of his self goes farther away from his self. It is necessary to understand this truthfully – then the search may even be possible.

If you want to find the material things of the world you have to look outside yourself. But if you want to find your self you have to drop all seeking and be composed, unruffled, unanxious. That which you are can only be found in total calm and emptiness. Remember that a search is also an anxiousness, a tension, a lust, a desire. But the self – the soul – cannot be realized through desire. This is the difficulty. Desire means that one wants to become something or to attain something, while the soul is that which is already attained. The soul is what I, myself, am. Desire and the soul are two opposite directions. They are opposite dimensions.

Hence, understand it well that the soul can be attained but it cannot become an object of desire. There cannot be any desire as such for the soul. All desire is worldly; no desire is spiritual. It is desire and lust that make up the world. Whether this desire be for money or for meditation, for worldly position or for godliness, for worldly pleasures or for liberation, it makes no difference. All desires are desires, and desire is a bondage.

I don't ask you to desire the soul. I only ask you to understand the nature of desire. The understanding of desire frees one from desire because it reveals its painful nature. The understanding of pain is freedom from pain because having understood it, no one can desire it. And in the moment when there is no desire, when the mind is not perturbed by lust and you are not searching for anything, then at that very moment, at that calm and tranquil moment you experience your real authentic being. The soul manifests itself when desire disappears.

Hence, my friends, I would ask you not to desire the soul but to understand desire itself and be freed from it. Then you will know and will realize the soul.

What is religion? Religion, dharma, has nothing to do with thoughts or with thinking. It has to do with no-thinking. Thinking is philosophy. It gives you conclusions but does not bring any solution. Dharma is solution. Logic is the doorway to thought while enlightenment is the doorway to solution.

Enlightenment is a contentless consciousness. The mind is empty but watchful, alert. In that peaceful state the door to truth opens. It is only in emptiness that truth is realized, and as a result one's whole life is transformed.

We reach this state of emptiness, this enlightenment,

through meditation. But what is generally understood as meditation is not really meditation. That too is a process of thinking. Maybe the thoughts relate to the soul or to the divine but they are still thoughts. It makes no difference what the thoughts are about. In fact thought by its very nature pertains to the other, to the outer. It relates to what is not the self. There can be no thought about the self because for thought to exist, two are needed. That is why thought does not take you beyond duality. If one is to move into and know non-duality – the self – then meditation is the way, not thinking.

Thought and meditation go in totally opposite directions. One is outward going; the other, inward going. Thought is the way to know the other; meditation, the way to know the self. But generally thought, contemplation, has been taken for meditation. This is a very serious and widespread mistake and I want to caution you against this fundamental error.

Meditation means to be in non-doing. Meditation is not a doing but a state of being. It is a state of being in one's own self.

In action we come into contact with the outside world; in no-action, with ourselves. When we are not doing anything we become aware of what we are. Otherwise, remaining involved in all sorts of doings we never get to meet ourselves. We don't even remember that we exist. Our busyness is very deep. Perhaps our bodies may get to rest but our minds never do. Awake, we think; asleep, we dream. Engrossed in these constant preoccupations and doings, we simply forget ourselves. We lose ourselves amidst the crowd of our own activity. How strange this is – but this is our reality. We have become lost, not in the crowds of other people, but in our own thoughts, in our own dreams, in our own preoccupations and activities. We have become lost in ourselves. Meditation is the way to extricate ourselves from this self-created crowd, from this mental wanderlust.

By its nature, meditation cannot be an activity. It is not a busyness, it is the term for an unoccupied mind. This is what

I teach. It looks rather odd to say that I teach non-doing, but this is what I teach. We have gathered here to practice non-doing. The language of man is very poor and very limited, designed to express action only; that is why it is never able to express the soul. How can what is tailored for speech express silence? The word *meditation* suggests that it is some sort of a doing but it is by no means a doing of any kind. It would be wrong to say "I was doing meditation"; it would be correct to say "I was in meditation." It is just like love. One can be "in" love, one cannot "do" love. Hence I say meditation is a state of mind. It is of prime importance to be clear about this from the very beginning.

We have gathered here to do nothing but experience that state where we simply exist – where no action takes place, where there is no impurity of action. It is a state where only the pure flame of being remains, where only the self remains, where even the thought that "I am" no longer remains, where simply "am-ness" remains. This is *shunya*, emptiness. This is the point where we see not the world, but truth. It is in this void, in this emptiness, where the wall that keeps you from knowing your self topples, where the curtains of thought rise and wisdom dawns. In this void there is no thinking, there is knowing. Here there is seeing; here there is vision.

But the words *vision* and *seeing* are also not appropriate because here there is no distinction between the knower and the known, no distinction between the subject and the object. Here there is neither the known nor the knower – simply the knowing. In this context no word is appropriate, only wordlessness. If anyone asks me about this state I remain silent – or I could say I convey my answer through my silence.

Meditation is non-doing. Doing is something we may do if we want to or may not do if we don't want to. But self-nature is not a doing. It is neither doing nor non-doing. For example, knowing and seeing are parts of our self-nature, parts of our being. Even if we don't do anything they will still be there. Self-nature is

constantly present in us. Only that which is constant and continuous in us is called self-nature. Self-nature is not something of our
creation, it is our foundation. We are it. We do not create it, we
are sustained by it. Hence, we call it dharma, that which sustains.
Dharma means self-nature; dharma means pure *isness*, existence.

This continuous nature of ours becomes suppressed in our
fragmentary stream of actions. Just as the ocean becomes covered by waves and the sun by clouds, we become covered by
our own actions. The layer of activities on the surface hides
that which is deep inside. Insignificant waves hide the ocean's
unfathomable depths. How strange it is that the mighty is suppressed by the trivial, that a speck in the eye makes mountains
invisible! But the ocean does not cease to exist because of the
waves. It is the very life of the waves and is present in them as
well. Those who know will even recognize the ocean in the
waves, but those who do not know must wait until the waves
subside. They can only see the ocean after the waves disperse.

We have to dive into this very self-nature. We have to forget
about the waves and jump into the ocean. We have to know our
own depths where there is *isness*, where there is ocean without
waves, where there is being, not becoming.

This world of waveless and motionless knowing is always
present in us, but we are not present to it. We have turned away
from it – we are looking outside, we are looking at things, we are
looking at the world. But bear one thing in mind: *we* are looking;
what is seen is the world, but the one who is seeing is not the
world, it is the self.

If seeing is identified with the object that is seen, it is
thought; if seeing is free from the object that is seen and turns
toward the seer, it is meditation. Do you follow my distinction
between thought and meditation? Seeing is present in both
thought and meditation but in the former it is objective and
in the latter it is subjective. But whether we are in thought or in
meditation, whether we are in action or in no-action, seeing is a

constant factor. Awake, we see the world; asleep, we see dreams; in meditation, we see ourselves – but in each of these conditions there is seeing. Seeing is constant and continuous. It is our nature. It is never absent no matter what the condition.

Seeing is even present in unconsciousness. After regaining consciousness one says, "I don't remember anything, I don't know where I was." Do not think that this is a not-knowing. This is also knowing. If seeing had been totally absent, then this knowing that "I don't know where I was" would not have been possible either. If that were the case, then the time that passed by while you were unconscious would have become nonexistent for you. In no way would it have remained a part of your life; it could not have left any trace on your memory. But you know you were in some state where you were not aware of any knowing. This too is a knowing; seeing is also present here. The memory has not recorded any internal or external phenomena happening during this period, but your seeing has definitely noted, has definitely experienced this gap, this interval. And this experience of the interval, of the gap in the recording of events, later becomes known to the memory as well. Similarly, during deep sleep when there are not even dreams, seeing is always present. When we wake up in the morning we are able to say we had such a sound sleep that we did not even dream. This condition too has been observed.

You must realize from all of this that situations change, that the object, the content for the consciousness changes, but that seeing does not change. Everything in the realm of our experience changes; all things are in a flux, seeing and seeing alone is ever-present. That alone is the witness to all this change, to all this flow. To realize this ever-present and eternal seeing is to know one's self. That alone is one's self-nature. All else is alien, the other. All else is *sansara*, the world.

This witness cannot be attained or realized by any doing, by any kind of worship or adoration, by any mantra or technique, because it is the witness of all those things as well. It is separate and apart from all those things. It is separate and different from all that can be seen or done. It cannot be realized by doing but by non-doing; not by action but by emptiness. It will be realized only when there is no activity, when there is no object to be seen, when only the witness remains, when only seeing remains.

When there is seeing but nothing to be seen, when there is knowing but nothing to be known, then in this contentless consciousness the knower of all is known. When there is no object to be seen, the curtain in front of the seer drops away, and when there is no object to be known, knowing emerges. When there are no waves, the ocean is seen; when there are no clouds, the blue sky is seen.

This ocean and this sky, this empty space is there within everyone and if we wish to know this sky, this space, we can. There is a path that leads there and that too is present within us all. And each one also knows how to walk on this path. But we know how to walk on it in only one direction. Have you ever thought of the fact that there can be no path that leads in one direction only? Each path inevitably goes in two directions, in two opposite directions. Otherwise it is not a path; it cannot exist. The path that has brought you here to the seclusion of these hills is the same path that will take you back. There is only one path for coming as well as for going. The same path will serve both purposes. The path will be the same but the direction will not be the same.

The path to *sansara*, the world, and the path to the self is one and the same. The same path leads either to *sansara* or to the self: only the direction changes. What has been in front of you so far will now be behind you and you will have to direct your attention to what was at your back. The road is the same, you must simply turn, do an about-face. You must turn your back on what you were facing and face that which was behind you.

Ask yourself where you are facing now. What are you seeing

now? In what direction is the current of your vision, of your consciousness flowing? Experience it. Observe it. You will find it is flowing outwardly. All your thoughts are about the outer. All the time you are thinking about the outer, about the world outside. When your eyes are open you see the outside. When you close them you still see the outside because the imprints of the outside forms and images surround you once again. There is a world of objects outside you; there is another world inside you, a world of thoughts – the echo of these outer things. Although it is found inside, this world of thoughts is still the outer because the "I" as a witness is also apart from it. Your "I" sees it as well, so therefore this world of thoughts is also outside.

We are surrounded by things and by thoughts. But on looking more deeply, you will find that it is not being encircled by things that hinders us on the path of self-realization, it is being encircled by thoughts. In the first place, how can things encircle the soul – matter can only encircle matter. Thoughts encircle the soul. The current of seeing, of consciousness, is flowing toward thoughts. Thoughts and thoughts alone are in front of us; our entire seeing is veiled by them.

We have to turn from thoughts toward thoughtlessness. This change of direction is the revolution! How can it be done? First we must know how thoughts are born and only then can they be stopped from being born. Generally seekers set about suppressing thoughts without bothering to understand the process of how they are born. This can certainly bring madness, but not liberation. The suppression of thoughts makes no difference because new thoughts are being born every moment. They are like those demons of mythology who, when one head was chopped off, grew ten more.

I don't ask you to kill thoughts because they go on dying each moment of their own accord. Thoughts are very short-lived; no thought endures for long. A particular thought does not endure, but the thought process does. Thoughts die on their own one after another, but the flow of thoughts does not. Hardly has one thought died before another one takes its place. This replacement is very quick, and this is the problem. The real problem does not concern the death of a thought but its quick rebirth. So I don't ask you to kill thoughts, I ask you to understand the process of their conception and be rid of it. One who understands the process of the conception of thoughts easily finds the path to be free of it. But one who does not understand the process goes on creating fresh thoughts and at the same time tries to resist them. Instead of thoughts coming to an end, the consequence is that the person who is fighting them breaks down himself.

Again I repeat: thoughts are not the problem, the birth of thoughts is the problem. How they are born is the question. If we can stop their coming into being, if we can exercise thought birth control, then the thoughts that have already been born will disappear in a moment. Thoughts are dying out every second, but their total destruction does not happen because new thoughts keep springing up continuously.

I want to say it is not that we have to destroy thoughts but that we have to stop their coming into being. Stopping their birth is their complete elimination. We all know that the mind is constantly in motion, changing. But what does this mean? It means that a thought doesn't live long. It only has a momentary life: it is born and it passes away. If we can only stop its birth, we will be saved from the violence involved in killing it and it will have ceased of its own accord.

How is thought born? The conception and birth of a thought is the result of our reaction to the outside world. There is a world of events and objects outside and our reaction to this world is alone responsible for the birth of thoughts. I look at a flower. Looking is not a thinking, and if I simply go on looking, no thought will arise. But as soon as we look at it we say, "It is a very beautiful flower," and a thought has been born. If on the other hand I merely look at the flower, I will experience its beauty, but no thought will be born. But as soon as we glimpse an experience we begin to give it words. As soon as an experience is given words, thought has taken birth.

This reaction, this habit of giving words to experience covers up the experience, the seeing, with thoughts. The experience is suppressed, the seeing is suppressed and only words are left floating in the mind. These words themselves are our thoughts. These thoughts are very short-lived so before one thought dies away we transform another experience into thoughts. This process continues throughout our lifetimes, and we become so filled with words and so burdened under them that we lose ourselves in them. To drop the habit of giving words to our experiences is to eliminate the birth of thoughts. Try and understand this.

I am looking at you, and if I just keep on looking at you without giving any word to this seeing, what will happen? As you are now you cannot even imagine what will happen. There will be such a great revolution in your life that it has no parallel. Words get in the way and stop that revolution from taking place. The birth of thoughts becomes a barrier to that revolution. If I keep on looking at you and do not give any words to it, if I simply keep on looking, I will find during the process that a peace from beyond this world is descending upon me and that an emptiness, a void is spreading all over, because the absence of words is the void.

In this emptiness, in this void, the direction of consciousness takes a new turning and then I do not see only you, but gradually the one who is seeing also begins to emerge. There is a new awakening on the horizon of one's consciousness, as if one is waking from a dream, and one's heart is filled with pure light and infinite peace. It is in this light that the self is seen. It is in this void that the truth is experienced.

Lastly, in this meditation camp, do not let your seeing be covered by words – this is what we will practice. I call this the experiment of right remembrance, right mindfulness. You must keep this remembrance, this awareness that words are not formulated, that words do not come in between. It is possible, because words are only our habit. A newborn child sees the world without the intermediary of words. This is pure, direct seeing. Later he gradually learns the habit of using words, because words are helpful and useful in his external life, in his outer life. But what is useful in the outer life becomes a hindrance to knowing the inner life. And that is why an old man must reawaken in himself the child's capacity of pure seeing in order to know his "self." He has known the world with the help of words, and now he must come to know his self with the help of the void, the emptiness.

What are you to do in this experiment? You will sit quietly, keeping the body relaxed and the spine erect. You will stop all movement of the body. You will breathe slowly and deeply and without any excitement. You will silently observe your own breathing. You will listen to any sounds coming to your ears from outside and you will not react to them in any way; you will not give them any thought. You will let go into a state of being where there are no words but only a witnessing: standing at a distance one is aware of whatever is going on. Do not concentrate on something. Simply go on remaining watchful and alert to whatever is happening.

Listen. Just close your eyes and listen. Listen quietly, in silence. Listen to the chirping of the birds, to the gusts of the winds swaying the trees, to the cry of a child, to the sound of the water wheel at the well. Simply listen, to the movement of the breath and to your heartbeat.

A new kind of peace and serenity will descend upon you. You will find that although there is noise outside there is silence inside. You will find you have entered a new dimension of peace. Then, there are no thoughts, only pure consciousness remains. And in this medium of emptiness your attention, your awareness turns toward the place that is your real abode. From the outside you turn toward your home.

It is seeing that has led you outward, it is seeing that will lead you inward. Simply keep watching. Watch your thoughts, your breath and the movement at your navel. No reaction to anything is needed. Then something happens which is not a creation of your mind, which is not your creation at all; rather your being, your *isness*, your intrinsic nature that sustains you is revealed and you find yourself face to face with the surprise of all surprises – your self.

I recall a tale:

A sadhu, a seeker, was once standing on a hill. It was early morning and the sun was beginning to shine. Some friends were out for a walk. They saw the sadhu standing all alone. They asked each other, "What can this sadhu be doing there?"

One of them said, "His cow sometimes gets lost in the jungle and perhaps he is standing on the hill looking for her." The other friends did not agree. Another said, "From the way he is standing, he does not seem to be looking for something. He rather seems to be waiting for somebody, perhaps a friend who accompanied him and has been left behind somewhere." But the others did not agree with this either. A third one said, "He is neither searching for anyone nor waiting for anyone. He is absorbed in the contemplation of God." They could not agree so they approached the sadhu himself to clarify the situation.

The first one asked, "Are you looking for your lost cow?" The sadhu replied, "No." Another asked, "Are you waiting for someone then?" To this he answered, "No." The third one asked, "Are you contemplating God?" Again the sadhu replied in the negative. All the three were amazed.

Together, they asked him, "Then what are you doing here?" The sadhu said, "I am doing nothing. I am just standing. I am just being."

We have just to exist this simply. We have to do nothing. We have to let go of everything and just be. Then something that cannot be put into words will happen. That experience alone which cannot be expressed in words is the experience of the truth, the self, of godliness.

CHAPTER 4

Meditation Is Non-Doing

Osho,
Is there a conflict between religion and science?

No. The knowledge of science is incomplete knowledge. It is as if there were light all over the world and in your own house, darkness. With such incomplete knowledge, without knowing one's own self, life simply turns into misery. For life to be filled with peace, contentment and fulfillment, it is not enough to know material things alone. That way one may find prosperity but not fulfillment. That way one may have possessions but one will not have light. And without light, without knowledge, possessions become a bondage – a self-made noose with which to hang oneself.

One who knows *only* the world is incomplete, and incompleteness brings misery. By knowing the world one gains power, and science is a search for that very power. Hasn't science put the secret keys to limitless power into mankind's hands already? Yes, but nothing worthwhile has come out of the attainment of that power: power has come but not peace. Peace comes by knowing godliness, not material things. This search for godliness is religion.

Power without peace is self-destructive. The knowledge of matter without the knowledge of the self means power in the hands of ignorance. No good can come of it. The conflict that has prevailed between science and religion, worldliness and spirituality so far has had disastrous results. Those who have searched only in the realm of science have become powerful but they are restless and anguished. And those who have searched only in religion have no doubt attained peace but they are weak and poor. Thus spiritual discipline so far has been incomplete and divided. So far there has been no complete and undivided search for truth.

I want to see power and peace in their undivided form. I want a synthesis, a meeting of science and religion. That will give birth to a whole man and to a whole culture, which will be rich both in the inner and in the outer. Man is neither only the body nor only the soul, he is a meeting of the two. Hence if his life is based only on one of the two it becomes incomplete.

Osho,
What is your opinion about *sansara*, the world and sannyas, the renunciation? Is sannyas only possible if one renounces the world?

There is no conflict between the world and sannyas. One has to renounce ignorance, not the world. Renouncing the world is not sannyas. The awakening of knowing, of self-realization, is sannyas. This awakening leads to a renunciation, not of the world, but of attachment to it. The world stays where it is and as it is, but we are transformed, our outlook is transformed. This transformation is very original. In this awakened state you do not have to give up anything. What is useless and superfluous drops on its own like the dry leaves from a tree. Just as the darkness disappears with the coming of light, so with the dawn of knowing, the impurities of life are swept away and what remains is sannyas.

Sannyas has nothing to do with the world. It has to do with the self. It is the purification of the self, just like the purification of impure gold. There is no contradiction between impure gold and pure gold but only a refinement. Looking at life from the standpoint of self-ignorance is *sansara*, the world. Looking at life from the standpoint of self-knowing is sannyas.

Therefore, whenever someone says to me that he has taken sannyas, the whole thing seems very false to me. This "taking" of sannyas creates the impression that it is an antagonistic act against the world. Can sannyas be taken? Can anyone say he has "taken" knowing? And will any knowing that is taken like that be true knowing? A sannyas that is taken is not sannyas. You cannot put a cloak of truth around you. Truth has to be awakened within you.

Sannyas is born. It comes through understanding, and in that understanding we go on being transformed. As our understanding changes, our outlook changes and our behavior is transformed without any effort. The world stays where it is, but sannyas is gradually born within us. Sannyas is the awareness that I am not only the body, I am also the soul. With this knowing, the ignorance and attachment inside us drops away. The world was outside and it will still continue to be there, but inside us there will be the absence of attachment to it. In other words, there will be no world, no *sansara* inside us.

To try to cling to the outside world is ignorance and to try to renounce it is also ignorance, because in both these states you continue to be related to it. Attachment and antagonism to the world are both ignorance. They both are relationships. The non-relationship is going beyond both. Non-attachment is not renouncing, it is the absence of both clinging and renouncing. This absence of clinging and renouncing I call sannyas.

Freedom from both attachment and renouncing comes

through knowing, through understanding. Attachment is ignorance, and the reaction that comes from being fed up with that attachment is renouncing. This reaction too is ignorance. In the first case a person runs toward the world; in the second case, away from it. But in both cases he runs and he does not know that bliss for the one enshrined within him is neither in running after the world nor in running away from it. The bliss is in being firmly settled in one's own self. One has neither to run toward the world nor from it. Rather one has to come within, to one's self.

Remember, we have to come into our selves. This coming home happens neither through attachment nor through renouncing. It only becomes possible by becoming a witness to the inner conflict between attachment and renunciation. There is one within us who is the witness to both our attachment and our renunciation. We have to know this witness. By knowing that which is only a witness, non-attachment happens on its own. This is a natural outcome of self-realization.

> Osho,
> According to you then, renunciation of home and family
> is useless.

I remember a sutra of Mahavira's. He said: "Unconsciousness is possession." He did not say that possession was unconsciousness. Why? It is because of our ignorance, because of our inner unconsciousness that we are attached to worldly objects. Inside we are empty and impoverished, so we want to fill ourselves with outward objects. That way we delude ourselves into believing we are important. If one gives up attachment under these conditions while ignorance remains within, can one really get rid of attachment? One will get rid of things but not of attachment.

One may leave his home for an ashram, but the attachment will shift to the ashram. One may leave his family, but his attachment will shift to the sect. As long as the attachment is there on the inside, it will find ways to manifest itself under any new condition. Hence, those who know have advised renunciation of unawareness, of ignorance, not of material objects. Once knowing dawns, the things that are futile do not have to be abandoned, they drop away on their own.

Osho,
Do we need to concentrate the mind in order to attain thoughtlessness?

I do not ask you to concentrate your mind. Concentration is a kind of forcing, a kind of tension. If one concentrates on some idea, on some form or image or on some word, it will lead neither to thoughtlessness nor to the awakening of consciousness but to an unconscious state of auto-hypnotic mental stupor. Forced concentration leads to unconsciousness. And it is an error to mistake this unconsciousness for *samadhi*, for no-mind. *Samadhi* is neither a state of unconsciousness nor of stupor. *Samadhi* is the realization of total consciousness. *Samadhi* is thoughtlessness plus total consciousness.

Osho,
How are we to watch the processes of incoming and outgoing breath in meditation?

Keep the spine erect. Make sure it is not bent. The body is in a state of natural balance when the spine is held erect. In that position the gravitational pull of the earth has a uniform effect on the body and it is easy to free oneself from that pull. When the force of gravity is at its minimum the body does not interfere in one's becoming empty, in one's becoming devoid of thoughts. Keep the spine erect, but without causing any tension or rigidity in the body. Allow the body to be naturally relaxed as if it were hung on the spine like a piece of cloth on a peg.

Leave the body relaxed. Then breathe slowly and deeply. The inhaling and the exhaling will move the naval center up and down. Continue to watch this movement. You don't need to concentrate on it, just watch it, be a witness to it. Bear in mind I am not asking for concentration. I am advising simple watchfulness and awareness. Breathe as children do – their chests do not move; their stomachs move. This is the natural process of inhalation and exhalation. As a result of this natural breathing, peace descends, becoming deeper and deeper.

Because of the disturbed and tense condition of our minds we have gradually lost the ability to breathe deeply and fully. By the time we grow to adolescence, superficial and artificial breathing becomes a habit. You must have noticed yourself that the more your mind is disturbed the more your breathing loses its natural and rhythmic movement. Breathe in a natural way – rhythmically, effortlessly. The harmony of natural breathing helps dispel the restlessness of your mind.

Osho,
Why do you advise us to observe the breathing process?

I do so because breathing, inhaling and exhaling, is the bridge between the body and the soul. The soul resides in the body through breathing and because of breathing. By becoming aware of your breath, by direct perception of breathing, you will gradually experience that you are not the body: "I am in the body but I am not the body alone. It is my abode but not my foundation."

As the direct perception of breathing deepens, more and more one experiences the presence, the proximity of the one who is not the body. There will come a moment when you will clearly see the separateness of your self and body. Then the three layers of your existence will be realized – the body, the breath and the soul. The body is the shell; the breath is the bridge, the connecting link; the soul, the self, is the foundation.

The role of the breath on the path to self-realization is the most important one, because breathing is the midpoint. On one side of it we have the body; on the other, the soul. We already exist on the body level; what we yearn for is to be in the realm of the soul. Before this can be done it is essential to be at the level of *prana*, the breath. The transition is through the breath.

Watching at the level of the breath, we can look both ways. From there the paths leading to the body and to the soul become clear. The path is one and the same, but the two directions stand out clearly. It then becomes easier to go on following the breath. I hope you now understand why my emphasis is on breathing.

Osho,
Why do you call meditation a non-doing? Is it not an act as well?

Look here, please. My fist is closed. To close my fist I must make a positive action. Closing is an action, a doing. But when I wish to open it, what must I do? I don't have to do anything to open it. If I simply drop the effort of closing the fist it will open on its own and the hand will return to its natural and normal state. Therefore I won't call opening one's fist a "doing." It is a "non-doing," or if you like you can call it "negative action." But that makes no difference; it is the same thing. I have no insistence about words, just that you can understand my point, my intent.

By calling meditation a non-doing, I wish to indicate that you should not regard meditation as a task or an occupation. Meditation is a state of non-occupation. It is a naturalness and you do not have to turn it into some kind of mental tension. If meditation were also a mental tension, a "doing," it would not lead you into your self-nature, into peace. Tension itself is a restlessness. And in order to enter the realm of peace one has to begin with peace. If there is no peace at the very first step, there will certainly be none at the last. The last is just the culmination of the first.

I see people going to temples and I see them worshipping gods and goddesses there. I also see them sitting in meditation, but it is all an activity, a tension, a sort of restlessness for them. And if they expect flowers of peace to bloom in this restlessness, they are utterly mistaken.

If you want peace, if you wish to be peaceful, it is essential that you start out in peace from the very first moment.

CHAPTER 5

Stop and See

Do not search for truth. In searching there is ego. And it is the ego itself that is the obstacle. Just lose yourself, disappear. When the "I" as the ego disappears, that which really is, is seen. When the "I-ness" disappears, the *isness* of "I" is seen. Only by losing oneself does one attain one's self. Just as new life sprouts from a seed only when the seed breaks apart and ceases to be, the shoot of immortal life springs up only when the seed called "I," which is a covering over the soul, breaks apart and ceases to be.

Remember this sutra: You have to disappear if you want to attain to self. Deathlessness is attained at the cost of death. A drop becomes the ocean when it loses itself in the ocean.

You are the soul, but if you search for it within yourself you will find nothing but desire. Our whole lives are desire. Desire means wanting to become something, to attain something. Everyone wants to become somebody, to attain something. This race goes on every moment of our lives. Nobody wants to be where he is. Everybody wants to be where he is not. Desire means a blind dissatisfaction with what is and a blind longing for what is not. There is no end to this mad race because as soon as one gets something it becomes useless and then desire centers again on what one does not have. Desire is always for the unachieved.

Desire is like the horizon. The more you try to approach it the farther it pulls away from you. This becomes possible because the horizon simply does not exist. It is just an appearance, an illusion. It is not real. If it were real it would come closer to you as you neared it; if it were unreal it would cease to be at your approach. But if it is neither real nor unreal, if it is an appearance, a dream, an illusion, a figment of the imagination, it will remain as far away as before, no matter how hard you try to get close to it.

Unreal is the opposite of real. Illusion, *maya*, is not the opposite of real but it is its veil, its cover. Desire is not the opposite of the soul but it is its veil, its cover. It is a fog, a smoke that hides our being, our soul. We keep running after what we are not and as a consequence we cannot see what we are. Desire is a veil on the soul and because of that it becomes impossible for us to know our souls. Because we constantly want to become something else, we never look at that which we are.

If this race, this desire to become something else ceases even for a moment, that which is manifests just as the sun manifests the moment the sky is cloudless. I call the absence of this race to become *dhyana*, meditation. And what a sense of wonder one experiences in the moment one knows that which really is, because in that moment everything one ever desired is attained. Seeing the soul is the total fulfillment of desire, because there is nothing lacking there.

Thought is a sign of ignorance. In knowing, there is no thought, there is only seeing. Hence the path of thinking never takes one to knowing. Consciousness – being free of thought – is the door to knowing. Knowing is not an achievement, it is a discovery. We don't have to achieve it, we have to uncover it. It is ever-present within us. We just have to dig it out as we dig out a well.

Fresh water springs, natural sources of water, lie buried

under layers of rock deep beneath the earth. As soon as these rocks are removed, the stream of water rushes out. I see layers of thought burying the sources of knowing. As soon as these thoughts are removed, we have a limitless stream of consciousness. Dig a well within yourselves. Remove the layers of thought with the tool of meditation. Make thoughts lifeless, make them rootless through right-mindfulness and alert awareness. What you will know then is knowing. In that pure flame of consciousness where there are no thoughts, is knowing.

I do not ask you to go into solitude. I ask you to create solitude within yourself. A change of place won't help, a change of your inner state is necessary. It is not the situation but the state of your mind that is the central and important point. You may go to a solitary place, but if there is no solitude within you, you will be surrounded by the crowd even there, for the crowd will be there inside you.

My friends, the crowd is not outside, it is within you. You are surrounded by the crowd within, so how will running away from the crowd outside help? The crowd that is with you now will go with you into your solitude. Running away from the crowd is useless. To disperse the crowd from within is the only meaningful thing. So, don't search for solitude outside, become a solitude. Don't go to a solitary place, create a solitary space within. The moment you experience yourself within, in your absolute aloneness, you will know that there has been no world, there never has been a world outside, it was all inside you. Seen out of peace, emptiness and solitude, this world turns into the divine. You find that you, yourself are all that which was surrounding you. *You* turn into all. It must have been in such a moment that someone exclaimed, *"Aham brahmasmi"* – I am God, I am the ultimate reality.

The dust of the ages lies heaped on our minds. Traditions, conventions and superstitions have covered us. Just as a deserted house is covered with spiders' webs and inhabited by the birds of darkness, in the same way we are full of thoughts borrowed from others. And these borrowed thoughts about truth and about God are great obstacles. They keep us from knowing the truth ourselves. So the stirrings of the search for the self that can awaken our sleeping consciousness never even start in us.

Before one can know truth for oneself, it is necessary to rid oneself of the knowledge borrowed from others. Brush off all this information taken from others, from traditions, as you would brush the dust from your hat. A cleanliness will arise, and the curtain between the truth and yourself will no longer be there. The crowd of thoughts stands in between like a wall.

There is a world of difference between knowing *about* the truth and knowing the truth. Knowing about the truth is a bondage of the borrowed, dead knowledge; knowing the truth is the free sky of self-experiencing. One takes away your ability to fly; the other gives you wings that can take you to the divine. It is because of this that I talk of emptiness, of nothingness.

Emptiness removes the burden of thought. Just as a man must leave his burden on the plain before climbing the mountain, one must be free from the burden of thought before setting out on the expedition to truth. The lighter a mountain climber is, the higher he will be able to climb. In the same way, one who wants to climb the mountain of truth will scale heights in direct proportion to his weightlessness, to his emptiness. Those who aspire to that ultimate peak, the divine, must reach that ultimate emptiness where their being becomes nonbeing. It is in the profound depths of emptiness where the absolute heights are born and the music of being is created out of nonbeing. And then one realizes that nirvana, cessation itself is the attainment of the *brahman*, the divine.

Truth is unknown. How can it then be known by thoughts which are a known thing? The effort is altogether absurd. There is no path that leads through the known to the unknown. The known cannot take you to the unknown. It is neither logical nor possible. The known can only revolve within the circle of the known. No matter how hard one thinks within the realm of the known there is no possibility of going beyond it or above it. It no doubt has movement but it is a circular movement, like that of a bullock yoked in a press. It will cover the same ground again and again without going anywhere.

So far nobody has ever reached the truth by thinking. Those who have reached that destination have gone through some other door. I do not consider Mahavira, Lao Tzu, Buddha or Jesus as thinkers. None of their attainments is the result of thinking. Then how did they reach? It was not by walking along the path of thinking but by taking a jump away from it. You cannot reach the unknown by walking along the beaten path of the known. It is a jump from the known that takes you into the unknown.

Try to understand the meaning of this word *jump*. Get to know this *jump* well. You too have to take it. You are at the level of thinking. You are standing in thought, you are living in thought and you have to take a jump from there into the realm of thought-lessness. You have to jump from thoughts into a world where there is nothing but silence. You will have to jump from word – which is sound – into silence. Will this be possible just by thinking about this jump? Are you going to think about how to take the jump? No, that will be nothing but yoking yourself again to the wheel of thought and that won't take you anywhere.

Don't think – wake up! Wake up to the process of thought. Look at the circular motion of thought. Simply watch. And watching this way you will find that at some moment the jump has happened without any effort and that you are in the bottom-less depths of emptiness. If somehow you can leave the shore of the known you will find that the sails of your boat have opened spontaneously on the ocean of the unknown. And what a joy it is to sail like this, to sail on the ocean of the unknown! How can I describe it?

Your restlessness does not allow you to see. Eyes that are filled with restlessness cannot see. Whether they are filled with tears of sorrow or tears of joy makes no difference. Eyes that are filled with anything cannot see the truth. To see the truth, eyes that are empty are needed. Only an eye that is like a mirror, with nothing of its own in it, can see that which is everything.

It happened in a village. Someone asked me how to find God. I asked him, "Have you found yourself and so now you want to set out to find God?"

We want to know God, but we don't even know our own selves, we don't even know what is closest to us! No other entity is closer to us than our own self – so ignorance can be defeated and destroyed only there. For one who is ignorant there, it is not possible to have first hand knowledge on any other level.

The flame of knowing begins to burn first in man's inner being. This inner being is "the east" of knowing; the sun of knowing rises there. If there is darkness there, you can be certain there cannot be light anywhere else. Know *yourself*, not God. This ray of light will ultimately grow into the sun. It is by knowing one's self that one realizes that there is *sat-chit-anand*, that there is being, consciousness and bliss, but that there is no "I," no ego. That very realization is the realization of godliness.

Man is a soul shrouded by an ego – and this is ignorance. A soul that is rid of the ego is God – and this is knowing. Where are you going in search of your soul? It is nowhere to be found in any of the ten directions. But there is one more direction, an eleventh. Do you know it? I will show you this direction.

You yourself are that eleventh direction and you can find this direction if you stop looking in the other ten. The eleventh direction is not like the other ten. In reality it is not a direction at all. It is no-direction, the negation of direction. It takes you where you have never left. It is your own entity, the state of your own self-nature. All of the ten directions go outward. What they create together is the world. The ten directions are the world.

They are the space, the gap. But the one that knows all of these directions and moves in them must certainly be separate from them, otherwise it could neither know them nor move in them.

It moves and at the same time it does not move because if it were not firmly still in its own *isness* it wouldn't be able to move. At the center of all its movement there is stillness, at the center of its revolving wheel there is a still point. Have you ever noticed the wheels of a carriage? The wheels are only able to move because the axle is stationary. There is always a fixed thing holding and sustaining any movement. Life is unstable and transitory, but the soul is permanent and stable. The soul is the eleventh direction. One does not have to go anywhere in search of it – simply nowhere. Drop all searching and see who resides in you. Wake up to the one who is. This is possible only by non-searching. It is possible only by stopping, not by running.

Stop and see. In these two words lies the crux of religion, of all spiritual endeavor and practice. Stop and see, and the eleventh direction opens up for you. Through it you enter the inner sky. That inner sky, that inner space is the soul.

I see that you are all running after something, but all this running ends in nothing but a fall. Don't you see people falling every day? Isn't that the result of all this running? Doesn't all this running end in death? Those who realize this truth early on are saved from that disaster at the end.

I want you to stop and see. Will you do it? In the unconsciousness of your frantic running do you hear my call? Stop and see who it is that is running. Stop and see who it is that is seeking. Stop and see who the "I" is. As soon as the fever of running subsides, all ten directions vanish and only that one direction, that no-direction, remains. It takes you to the root, to the source, to the very origin.

A master used to ask people what they were like before they were born. If you meet that master, what will you say to him? Do you know what you were like before you were born? Do you know what you will be like after your death? If you learn to stop and see, you can know. That which was there before birth, that which will be there after death is there inside you now at this very moment. It is just a matter of turning around a little and looking. Stop and see.

I invite you to travel into this wonderful world.

CHAPTER 6

Naturally Moral

Conscious soul,

I quite understand your longing and your eagerness. You are eager to know and to understand the truth. You want to unfold the mystery of life so that you can attain to it. What we now call life is not really life at all. It can only be called a long, drawn-out process of dying. It is true that one cannot attain life without knowing it. Birth is one thing, life is quite another. There is a vast difference between having been born and the attainment of life. The difference is as great as that between death and immortality. The end of just managing to stay alive is in death, while the completeness of life is in a life that is divine, godly.

For those who become eager for a divine life, who want to know God and truth, it seems to me there are two directions of approach, two paths. One is the approach of morality; the other, of religion. Morality and religion are not usually viewed as two different paths. They are regarded as two successive steps on the same ladder. It is generally believed that for a man to become religious he must first become moral. But this is not so as I see it.

I will tell you what I have known. I do not find that a moral man is essentially a religious man although a religious man is invariably moral. One does not become religious merely by becoming moral, nor is morality the starting point or the basis of religion. On the contrary, morality is the result of becoming religious – the flowers of morality blossom on the plant of religion. Morality is the expression of a religious life. I look upon religion and morality as two different directions – not only different but opposite to each other. I would like to explain it to you.

Discipline, morality means the purification of conduct, the purification of behavior. It is an attempt to change man's personality on the periphery. The periphery of the personality is the result of our relationships with others. It is one's behavior, one's relations with others. How I behave or act with others is my behavior. Behavior is a relationship.

I am not alone; I am surrounded by people on all sides. And since I am in a society, I come into contact with and have relations with someone or other every moment of my life. These interrelationships seem to make my life. And the goodness or badness of my conduct is defined by whether my relationships are good or bad.

We are taught good conduct. It is the need of the society, it is a social necessity. But society has no interest in your own individuality, in your bare individuality. In that area, even if you don't exist it is of no consequence to society. You become important to society only the moment you relate with someone or something. It is not you but your behavior that is valuable to the society. It is not you but your behavior that is meaningful to the society. So it is not surprising if good conduct is the teaching of society. To the society, man is nothing more than his conduct.

But this teaching of good conduct, this commandment of morality by the society creates a fallacy. It has given birth to a very fundamental fallacy. Naturally those eager to realize God and religion believe that it is necessary to become virtuous for this attainment of truth. They believe that the realization of God is only possible through right conduct and that one must acquire virtue before the advent of truth. They believe that the realization of religion will develop only out of a life of morality, that morality is the basis and religion will be its peak, that morality is the seed and religion will be its fruit, that morality is the cause and religion will be the effect. This line of thinking seems to be clear and correct. But I want to say to you that this apparently simple and clear line of thinking is totally false and sees reality in an upside down posture. The truth of the matter is something quite different.

The way of morality doesn't even really make a man moral, let alone religious. It merely makes a man social, and being social is wrongly taken for being moral. Mere good behavior does not make a man really moral. That revolution requires an inner purification. Without transforming your inner being you cannot change your conduct. To try to change the periphery without changing the center is hoping in vain. The effort is not only futile, it is fatal. It is a violence to oneself. It is nothing but forcing affliction on oneself.

No doubt this suppression fulfills the needs of society, but the individual cracks under it and is shattered. It creates a rift, a duality in him. His being loses its naturalness and simplicity, and this turns into an inner conflict. It becomes a continuous struggle, an endless internal fight that can never become a victory. This is satisfying the needs of society at the cost of the individual. I call this social violence.

Whatever manifests itself in man's behavior is unimportant. The important things are the inner causes due to whom they are manifesting. Behavior is an indication of the inner, it is not the root. Behavior is only an outer manifestation of the inner being. Only ignorant people try to change the manifestation without changing the manifester.

That kind of spiritual endeavor is useless; it can never bear fruit. It is like someone wanting to kill a tree by cutting off its branches. Such an action, instead of killing the tree only promotes its foliage. The life of a tree is not in its branches, it is in its roots, in the unseen roots buried in the earth. It is the latent hopes and desires of the roots that have manifested in the form of the tree and its branches. How will cutting the branches help? If you really want to bring about a revolution in life you must go to the roots. The roots of man's behavior are in his inner being. Behavior follows the inner being, it does not precede it. Hence, any effort to change behavior can never become anything other than suppression. And can suppression bring about any transformation?

What is suppression anyway? Suppression is not allowing spontaneous feelings and behavior to arise from our inner being; it is forcibly bringing out and expressing what is not really there.

But where will what we suppress go? Will we become free of it this way? How can freedom come out of suppression? The suppressed things will continue to be there within us, but they will now have to find deeper, darker and more unconscious recesses in which to live. They will enter still deeper regions. They will hide themselves where even our awareness of suppression will not be able to locate them. But these roots that have gone deep will continue to sprout, the branches will blossom and bear fruit, and then there will be such a conflict between our conscious and unconscious minds that the ultimate result will be insanity.

Insanity is the natural outcome of a civilization based on this kind of false, so-called morality. Hence, insanity increases with the advance of civilization and the time may come when our whole civilization will end in insanity. The last two great wars were this kind of madness and we are preparing for a third, perhaps the final.

The explosions that happen in a man's personal life and those that occur in society – violence, rape, immorality, brutality – are all the results of suppression. A man cannot lead a simple and natural life because of suppressions, and one day he simply succumbs to the tension. No doubt those who resort to hypocrisy save themselves from this inner conflict. They pretend to be what they are not. They are not in an inner conflict, they are acting things out.

Hypocrisy too is born out of morality based on suppression. That too is an offspring of the so-called morality. It is a means of keeping oneself free of inner conflict. As I have already said, in our so-called moral lives we do not allow spontaneous behavior to arise from within and be expressed, and we express what is not really there. The first of the two processes leads to suppression; the second, to hypocrisy. The final outcome of the first process is a madman; and of the second, a hypocrite. Neither of the two outcomes is any good; neither is worth choosing. Our civilization offers only these two alternatives. But there is a third alternative as well: living the life of an animal. The criminal is born out of this alternative. We wish to avoid that, we wish to avoid becoming animals, so our civilization offers only the first two alternatives.

Becoming an animal means complete surrender to unconscious instincts. This too is impossible, because what has become conscious in man cannot become unconscious again. We seek this very unconsciousness in intoxication. The search for intoxicants is an indication of our desire to become animals. Only in a thoroughly unconscious state can man be in full conformity with nature, with the animal. But this is equivalent to death. This truth deserves our very careful consideration.

How does man, in a thoroughly unconscious state, become animal-like and why does he seek an unconscious state in order to become animal-like? It is indicative of the truth that consciousness in man is not part of the animal world, of nature, but is a part of the divine. It is a potential. It is a seed, not to be destroyed but to be nurtured. Only with its full growth is there the possibility of freedom, liberation and bliss.

Then what shall we do? Our civilization gives us three

alternatives: that of the animal, that of the madman and that of the hypocrite. Is there also a fourth alternative?

Yes, I call that fourth alternative religion. It is the path of intelligence, of consciousness – not of bestiality, madness or hypocrisy. It is not the path of indulgence, suppression or acting; it is the path of real life and of knowing.

It bears the fruit of good conduct and it eliminates the animal in man; it does not suppress unconscious passions but frees man from their grip. It does not lead to the pretense of good conduct but to real living. It is not assuming a mask or any outward behavior; it is the transformation of the inner being. It is not a solution of the society but of the self. It does not change our relationships but transforms our very selves. Relationships automatically change as a consequence. It brings about a revolution in our being, in our bare individuality, in what we actually are. Then all else is automatically transformed.

Morality is social; religion, entirely individual. Morality is behavior; religion, the inner being. Morality is the periphery; religion, the center. Morality is personality; religion, the soul. Religion does not follow on the tail of morality but morality invariably follows religion. Morality cannot even succeed in making a man moral, so how can it make him religious? Morality begins with suppression, with holding things down in oneself, whereas religion begins with knowing.

There is evil, impurity and untruth in life. Man has to find his roots. Where and how is evil born? Where is the center in us from which these poisons erupt and make our behavior venomous? Even when we thinks of virtue, of good, why does evil drive away all these thoughts and engulf us, surrounding our life, permeating our behavior? Why does the power of passion always defeat our thoughts of the good?

We have to observe all of this for ourselves. Conclusions borrowed from others do not help because it is during the process of observation, during self-observation alone, that the power and energy to destroy the very source that breeds and sustains evil is generated. One has to practice this continuous observation oneself because it is not just a method of knowing about evil, but of eliminating it as well. By observing the "I," the inner unconsciousness, by becoming awake and watchful toward it, light reaches one's dark recesses within. And this light not only exposes the roots of one's behavior, it begins to transform them.

This sutra deserves your total attention: Observation not only creates knowing, it transforms as well. Actually, observation brings knowing and knowing brings transformation. The revolution of knowing is one's life transformed. It is just like digging away the earth and exposing all the roots of a tree to light in order to know them. Not only will this enable the roots to be known, but bringing them out of the darkness and separating them from the earth will be their death as well. On one hand I will be observing the roots of the tree, on the other hand the branches will be withering away.

Observation can become the death of the roots of desire and passion. They cannot bear light. Evil cannot endure knowing. When Socrates said, "Knowing is virtue," he most likely meant to convey this very thing. I also say the very same thing: Knowing is virtue; ignorance is evil. Light is real morality; darkness, immorality.

Observation, the constant observation of oneself, of the mind's unconscious tendencies, awakens the consciousness and allows it to penetrate into the unconscious mind. The unconscious enters the conscious through the door of stupor, unawareness, intoxication and carelessness, and overpowers it. We have seen that animalistic instincts and tendencies become possible only in unawareness. Anger and lust grab hold of us only when we are unconscious and that is the reason intoxicants help in satisfying our animal instincts.

Consciousness enters the unconscious mind through overcoming stupor, through vigilance, watchfulness and awareness.,

Consciousness overpowers it. To the degree that watchfulness and awareness grow in us, and to the degree that right-mindfulness and observation of our tendencies, actions, passions and desires develop in us, is to the same degree that consciousness fills us. And those drives and outbursts of passion, those blind, unconscious impulses disappear because they can only exist in a state of unawareness, sleep, and unconsciousness. They simply cannot exist in a state of consciousness.

Bear in mind that to date nobody has ever done anything wrong while aware, while conscious. All sin is born out of unawareness, it is unawareness itself. As I see it, unawareness is the only sin. Observation destroys unawareness. So let us understand what observation is and how it can be brought about.

What is self-observation then? It is sitting quietly – just as I explained yesterday when we discussed the experiment in right-mindfulness – and observing, watching whatever happens within us. There is a world of thoughts and passions inside. One observes that world; keeps on looking at it just as one stands on the seashore looking at the waves. Krishnamurti has called this "choiceless awareness." It is completely indifferent observation. To be indifferent is very necessary.

Indifference means making no choice, no judgment. One does not label any passion or desire as good or bad. One does not make any judgment of good and evil, between virtue and vice. One simply observes. One simply becomes a witness, standing aloof and apart, as if one has no other purpose than that of remaining aware and observing. The moment purpose creeps in, the moment choice or judgment comes in, observation comes to an end. Then I am not observing; then I have begun to think.

Try to understand the difference between thinking and observation. In this process we are not to think. Thinking is the action of the conscious within the conscious. Observation is the penetration of the unconscious by the conscious. As soon as thinking comes in, the distinction of good and evil comes in and a subtle suppression starts. The unconscious then closes its doors and we are deprived of knowing its mysteries. The unconscious reveals its secrets not to thought but to observation, because in the absence of suppression its impulses and tendencies surface naturally, spontaneously, in their total nakedness and reality, and there remains no need to dress them up to hide them. The unconscious stands before us in its nakedness, completely uncovered. And what terror it causes! How frightened a man is when he sees the naked form that resides deep in his own self. He feels like closing his eyes to it. He feels like abandoning this observation of the depths and running back to the surface.

This is the moment when one's patience and tranquility are put to the test. This, I call the moment of a quantum leap. Those who pass through this moment with courage and calmness become masters of a wonderful knowledge and mystery. They have seen the roots of desire and passion and they enter the very heart of the unconscious. This entry brings an otherworldly freedom.

From right awareness to observation, from observation to knowing, from knowing to liberation – this is the path. This is the path of religion, this is meditation. I want you to understand this path and to walk along it. Only then will you understand the alchemy of the transformation of behavior through inner revolution. Then you will see that morality does not come first. First comes religion, morality is its outcome. It is not morality but religion that is to be accomplished. Morality follows in the wake of religion as the tracks of the wheels of a bullock-cart follow the cart. If this becomes clear to you, you will see a very great truth, and a great illusion will be dispersed.

I see the transformation of man's life through this inner revolution, through this penetration of the unconscious by consciousness. On the basis of this science a new man can be born and the foundations of a new humanity and a new culture can be laid.

Such a man, one who has been awakened with self-realization, is naturally moral. He does not have to cultivate morality. It is not the result of his effort and his endeavor. It radiates from him as light radiates from a lamp. His good conduct is not based on an opposition to his unconscious mind but comes out of the totality of his inner being. He is totally present in each of his acts. There is no multiplicity in him, but unity. Such a man is whole, integrated; such a man is free of duality.

And the music one hears when one has gone beyond all inner duality is neither of this world nor of this time. A timeless immortal music penetrates us in that peace, in that non-duality, in that innocence, and we become one with it.

To me, this realization is godliness.

CHAPTER 7

Seeing without Thinking

Osho,
Do you think it is a bad thing to be moral?

No. I do not consider it bad to be moral but I do consider the illusion of being moral bad. It becomes an obstacle to real morality arising in you.

False morality is an outer imposition, a cultivation. It serves no purpose other than satisfying hypocrisy and in my view there is no state of mind that is more immoral than that of hypocrisy and egoism. False morality even covers itself up with a display of humility and of freedom from egoism, but beneath it the ego is being nourished and it flourishes. Do you not see the truth of what I am saying in your so-called saints and monks? I call this so-called morality – imposed from outside, cultivated by effort – nothing but an act. Often things in a man's inner mind are just the opposite. What appears on the surface is missing inside. There are flowers above and thorns below. And this continuous opposition and struggle between behavior and the inner being – an unbridge-able gap between consciousness and unconsciousness – divides and makes him schizophrenic. In such a man there is no harmony. And where there is neither harmony nor music there is no bliss. In my view, a real moral life is an expression of bliss.

Morality is an expression of bliss, a spontaneous expression. When bliss flows from one's inner being it is expressed in good conduct, in morality on the outside. The fragrance of bliss that emanates from such a man is the goodness of his life.

Hence I ask you to create harmony, not conflict. Try to see this truth. Do not just listen to what I say but try to live it. Only then will you see how with your own hands you turn your life, which could be one continuous dance of harmony and beauty, into an anarchy of conflict and inner duality.

Morality comes of its own accord – just as flowers appear on a tree. It is not brought about. The seeds of meditation need to be sown, and then the crop of morality is harvested. Morality is not something to be practiced; it is meditation that is to be practiced. Peace, harmony and beauty flow from meditation. And the one who is peaceful within himself becomes incapable of making others restless. The one who has music within him finds the echo of this music reverberating in others in his presence. The one who has beauty within him finds that all ugliness disappears from his behavior. Isn't becoming all this becoming moral?

Osho,
You say that morality is a social utility. Is it quite useless to the individual?

Morality or moral behavior is simply utilitarian as far as society is concerned, but for the individual it is not a utility, it is his joy. Therefore, society's needs are satisfied even by pseudo-morality, but that is not good enough for the individual. That you behave well toward others is good enough for society but it is not good enough for you, for it is also worth considering whether you are good inside yourself or not. Society is concerned with your personality, not with your inner being. But for you yourself the personality is nothing more than your clothing. Your being begins where this clothing ends. Behind this mask of personality, separate from it, is your real being. And this is where real morality is born.

A society created by false morality is called a civilization. A society consisting of men who have attained to real life is called a culture. This is the difference between civilization and culture. Civilization is based on utility; culture is based on inner joy and harmony.

Today we have civilization but not culture. But if we want, we can give birth to a culture with our individual efforts together. Civilization is born out of purifying our behavior with other people; culture is born out of purifying ourselves. Civilization is the body; culture is the soul. Those who are rooted in their beings create a culture.

Osho,
But isn't religion social? Is it totally personal?

Yes, religion is absolutely personal. Society has no soul, no center of consciousness as such. Society is simply an accumulation of our interrelationships. It is the individual who has a soul and therefore religion must be individual as well. Religion is not one of my relationships, it is my being. The discovery of what one is in one's intrinsic nature, in one's real *isness*, is religion.

Religion, dharma, is self-knowledge. Religion itself is not social. This means one's *sadhana* for religion, one's search and endeavor for religion, does not relate to any group or crowd. But one's religious experience does cast its light on the group, on society. The practice of religion is personal, but its effect does touch the society. When a man is filled with inner light his behavior also fills with it. The inner being is individual, personal, but behavior is social.

Spiritual growth can never be collective, because one has to come to know one's self not in the company of others, but alone, all alone. Plotinus has said: "It is the flight of the alone to the alone." It is quite true. The flight is indeed very alone, companionless. But the bliss that comes from the flight infects others and they are also moved. What is attained in aloneness, in the aloneness of one's self, spreads its fragrance far and wide.

Osho,
What is God?

God is not a person, it is an experience. The vision, the experience one has of the universe, of existence, after the dissolution of the ego-center, is what I call "God." There is no specific experience of God as a person; rather the experience of an all-pervading love is God. It has no center; it is the whole existence. The entire existence is its center. It is incorrect to call it "the experience of God," but you can say "the experience of all-pervading love is God."

Love is the relationship between two persons. When this relationship happens between an individual and the whole, I call it "God." The ultimate state of love, the perfection of love, is God. I am reminded here of a saying of Christ's: "God is love."

When the "I" disappears, what remains is love. When the walls surrounding the ego crumble, what remains is love. And that love itself is also "God." Hence, one cannot know God but one can become God.

Osho,
You said that this life we live is not life at all, but a long drawn-out process of dying. What do you mean to convey by this?

It is quite true that what we call life is not life. If it really were life how could it end in death? Life and death are two contradictory things so how then can death be the final outcome of life? Death is the end of birth, not of life.

And because death comes at the end don't think it really comes at the end. It is present in birth itself. It starts the very day one is born. After birth we die every moment. When this process of dying has been completed we call it death. What was present in birth as a seed appears at the end in its fully ripened form. Hence, although nothing else is certain after birth, death for sure is. It is certain because it arrives with birth itself. Birth is just another name for death; it is the seed of death. Let this be carefully understood. You begin dying the day you are born. That is why I say that life as we know it is not life but only a long, slow, gradual process of dying.

Because we become familiar only with this gradual dying and not with life, we are busy the whole time trying to save ourselves from it. All our plans and activities are aimed at some sort of security and self-defense. And what are we doing? Aren't we busy defending ourselves against death all the time? Man even becomes religious for the same reason – in defense. It is because of this that he takes to religion when he senses death drawing near. For the most part, the religion of old people is of this type. I don't call this real religiousness. It is just an aspect of the fear of death. It is the last safety measure. Real religiousness does not come out of a fear of death, but out of experiencing life.

We should be aware that whatever we know at present is nothing but death – and it is this knowing about death that leads to immortality. The body dies, it is dying each moment, but becoming aware of this body, by waking up to an awareness of this mortal vessel, we begin to experience that which is not the body. To know that which is not the body, is to know life in its reality; and because it is never born it never dies. This reality existed before your birth and it will continue to exist after your death. This is life. Life is not a span between birth and death –

on the contrary, birth and death are just episodes within it.

During meditation, when the mind is quiet and empty, something that is different and apart from the body is seen. It is not seen when the mind is restless, just as one cannot look into the depths of a lake when there are ripples on the surface. And so, because of the continuous current of thought-waves rippling on the mind, what is hidden under them remains hidden – and we take the surface to be the whole truth. The body, which is only one's dwelling place, seems to be all and everything. It creates the illusion that the body is one's whole existence and life. One takes oneself to be just the body and nothing more. This identification with the body, this illusion of being one with the body does not allow us to know the real life, and we look upon the gradual process of dying that is taking place within the realm of time as life. This is the same kind of mistake you would make if you looked upon the construction and destruction of your house as your own birth and death.

This darkness disappears with the advent of peace and tranquility of the mind. The illusion created by mental unrest is dispelled by tranquility. What was hidden by the waves is revealed by wavelessness. And then for the first time we know the inhabitant of this house called the body. As soon as we know this inhabitant, death stops being anything more than the casting off of old clothes, and birth a putting on of new ones. And then the life which is transcendental to all clothes is known. The only man I call alive is one who knows this kind of life, otherwise all else are dead. Those who have taken the body to be their being are all still dead. Their real lives are yet to begin. They are in a dream, asleep, in a fainting stupor.

Without waking from this unconsciousness – without waking from this unconsciousness about the body – man will never be able to know his own self, his being, his basis, his very life. The world is full of the dead, the living dead, and the majority of people die without ever having lived. They become busy only in protecting themselves against death and in this busyness they never come to know that which is within them, that which is deathless, that which never dies.

Osho,
Hearing your words I can see that I am dead. What should I do to find life?

My friend, if you see only because of my words it is of no value. Let go of words – mine and others as well – and then look. You should be able to see it yourself. That seeing itself will become a path leading you to life and then you won't have to ask, "What should I do to find life?"

He who comes to realize that he is dead, that his existence and his personality have been dead all along, will at the same time begin to see that which has no death. But in order for you to see this, the restlessness of your mind must disappear. Seeing, *darshan*, is only possible when the mind is quiet, empty, free of thought. At present there are only thoughts, there is no seeing whatsoever. That my words appealed to you, is a thought in itself. This thought will not help at all.

Thinking cannot uncover truth because all thoughts are borrowed. All thoughts belong to others. They just hide the truth all the more. Have you ever realized that all your thoughts are borrowed from others, that they really belong to others? You have amassed counterfeit capital. Do not depend on it because it is not capital at all. Castles built on this kind of capital are like the ones you build in dreams. They are not even as real as houses of cards.

I don't want to give you any thought. I don't want to fill you with borrowed things. I don't want you to think but to awaken. I want you to let go of thinking and see. Then watch what happens. Move from thinking to seeing. This alone will take you to the truth and to the real capital, to the real wealth that is your own. How this process of seeing-without-thinking removes the curtain from the mystery cannot be known without actually doing it yourself.

Remember, there is no valuable experience in the world others can give you. Whatsoever can be given by others is neither valuable nor an experience. Only material things can be given, taken, but there is no way to give or take live experiences. Neither Mahavira, nor Buddha, nor Krishna, nor Christ – no one can give you anything. Those who cling to their thoughts and consider them as the truth are the ones who remain deprived of knowing the truth themselves. It is one's own experience of truth that liberates, not that of others.

Memorizing the Gita, the Koran or the Bible will serve no purpose. It will not bring you knowing. On the contrary, it will cover up your own capacity for self-knowing and you will never be able to stand face to face with truth. The words you have memorized from the scriptures will always come between you and the truth. They will create fog and dust and it will be impossible for you to see that which is. It is a must that you remove everything that stands between you and the truth.

To know the truth no help is required from thought. Strip everything away and then you will open up, then there will be an opening through which truth will enter you and transform you. Give up thinking and see. Open the door and see. This is all I say.

Osho,
Is the study of the scriptures not necessary then?

What purpose will the study of the scriptures serve? You can't attain to knowing that way, it just trains your memory. You learn a few things that way, but are learning and knowing the same thing? You learn about God, about truth, about the soul. You will be able to give ready-made answers about them. But there is no difference between that and what the parrot in your house repeats every morning. Truth is not to be found in the scriptures. It is in the self, in your self.

In scriptures, there are only words and they are meaningful only if one has realized the truth within oneself. Otherwise they are not only useless, they are harmful. Truth cannot be known by learning the scriptures, but certainly by knowing the truth the scriptures become known.

But what do I see before me? People are trying to know scriptures instead of the truth and are even feeling satisfied with the information they have gained. What a hollow and false satis- faction! Doesn't it suggest that we really don't want to know the truth, that we only want people to believe we know the truth? Anyone who really wants to know the truth can never be satis- fied with mere words. Have you ever heard of a man's thirst being quenched by the word *water*? And if it were quenched by a simple word, wouldn't that indicate there really hadn't been any thirst there at all?

Scriptures are only useful if they can make it clear to us that the truth cannot be realized through them. If the word can only tell us that the word is useless it will have served its purpose. It will be enough if the scriptures do not bring us contentment but create discontent in us, and if instead of giving us knowledge they make us aware of our ignorance.

I too am speaking in words, and this is how the scriptures came to be. If you just cling to the words, my whole effort will be useless. No matter how many of them you memorize, they will serve no purpose. These too will become a prison to your mind and then you will wander in this self-erected prison of words all your life. We are all locked in prisons of our own making. If you want to know the truth, destroy this prison of words, tear down the prison walls and burn the blockade of information to ashes. From these ashes real knowledge will be born and in this unimprisoned consciousness you will see truth. Truth comes, but before that you must make room for it in yourself. If you throw words out, truth steps into that empty space.

> Osho,
> Can't man ever conquer himself by suppression and by fighting with himself?

What do you mean by the words "suppression" and "fighting with himself"? Don't they mean that the individual will be dividing himself? He will be fighting with himself. This means he will be the attacker and the defender both. He will be both friend and enemy. His energy will be used by both sides. This will never lead to victory, it will only weaken him and shatter his strength. Imagine what will happen if I make my two hands fight with each other. The same will happen if I fight with myself. Such a fight is sheer foolishness.

My friend, you are not to fight with yourself, you are to know yourself. The contradictions and the self-conflicts that have been born in us out of ignorance of the self will disappear in the light of self-knowledge, just as the drops of dew on the grass evaporate with the sunrise in the morning. Victory over oneself comes through knowing, not through any conflict, for there is nobody there to be defeated. There is no other, only ignorance. What is there to defeat in ignorance? It vanishes the moment knowledge comes. By its nature ignorance is only an absence, an absence of knowledge. He who fights with ignorance fights with a shadow. He is walking the path of failure from the very beginning.

This concept of fighting to conquer oneself is a reflection of the fights between enemies in the outer world. We want to commit violence in our inner world just as we commit violence against our enemies in the outer world. What madness this is! Even in the outer world violence has never conquered anyone. To defeat is a very different matter.

But in the inner world we cannot even use violence to defeat our so-called enemy because there is no other there to be defeated. Self-conquest is not the result of fighting, it is the result of knowing. So I say: Do not fight, know. No war, only knowing.

And let this be the sutra: Uncover and know yourself. Let there be nothing in you that remains unknown to you. Let there not be a single corner in you that remains dark and uninspected. If you become familiar with all your inner rooms, that same familiarity turns into self-conquest.

We are all aware that in dark houses, in corners and in cellars inaccessible to sunlight and to fresh air, snakes, scorpions and bats make their abode. If the owners of these houses spend their lives outside of them, never entering, is it then surprising or unnatural that their houses are reduced to such miserable states? This is what has happened to us. We are also the owners of such houses and we have even forgotten where the doors to enter are. Because of our continued absence and the lack of light, only our enemies have taken up residence there.

Osho,
You say that the suppression of one's passions is harmful. Do you then mean to say that indulging them is the proper course?

I teach neither suppression nor indulgence. I teach to know the passions. Suppression and indulgence are both ignorance, both are injurious. Suppression is just a reaction to indulgence, only the inverted form of it. It is only indulgence placed upside down. It is not too different from indulgence. It is the same thing standing on its head.

Someone told me about a sannyasin who turns his face away from money. Is turning one's face away much different from one's mouth watering at the sight of money? The same thing will happen if you try to run away from greed. Greed will not cease to be, it will take another form. And the big problem is that in this other form it will be as strong as ever – and more secure because now it is invisible to you. It will remain intact, and in addition the illusion of there being no greed will have entered. This is like inviting another enemy in, while trying to drive one out.

I want you to know lust and to know anger. You are not to fight with them nor are you to follow them blindly. You should become aware. You should observe them and become well acquainted with them in all their forms and with all their mechanical processes.

Have you ever noticed that anger disappears when you watch it? But you immediately begin to indulge it or to suppress it. In either case, you fail to watch it. It remains unseen and unknown. This is where we make the mistake, and both indulgence and suppression support this error.

Apart from these two, there is a third alternative as well. And that is what I would like to suggest to you. It is to see, to observe your tendencies, your desires. Not to do anything with them, simply to watch them. Once they are under your watchfulness you will find they start dispersing and disappearing. They cannot stand being observed. Their existence is only possible in a state of unconsciousness. Under watchful consciousness they become lifeless and die. Our unconsciousness, our non-observation of them is their life. They are like insects who live only in darkness. As soon as there is light they die away.

CHAPTER 8

I'm a Dream-Breaker

What I am in others views is not significant. What is significant is what I am in my own view. But we are in the habit of seeing ourselves through other people's eyes and we forget that there is a direct and immediate way to see ourselves. And this alone is the real way to see because it is not indirect. So firstly we create false images of ourselves and wear masks to deceive others, and then we base our opinion of ourselves on how others see us!

This self-deception goes on throughout our lives. To begin a life of religiousness, the very first thing that needs to be shattered is this self-deception. It is necessary to break through all self-deceptions; it is necessary to know yourself in your total nakedness – as you are, what you are – because only after this has been done can any steps be taken in some authentic direction of self-realization.

Man cannot enter the realm of truth as long as he has false conceptions about himself and as long as the delusion persists that the role-playing personality is his real self. Before we can know God, or the truth or our real beings, we must reduce to ashes the imaginary personality with which we have covered ourselves. This mask of deception does not allow us to rise above the artificial lives we are acting out and live real lives. Those who wish to walk the path of truth, of reality, must awaken from the false drama they are living.

Don't you ever feel you are acting, performing in a drama? Don't you ever feel you are one thing on the inside and quite another on the outside? In some conscious moment, when you are yourself, doesn't the awareness of this deception ever trouble you? If questions about it do occur to you and do trouble you, that alone is the possibility that can take you out of the drama, can take you from the stage to the background, where you are not acting a role but are your own self.

One must ask oneself this question: "Am I really what I have been thinking I am?" This question must echo in the very depths of your being. It must arise in your depths with such intensity and such awareness that there remains no room left for the possibility of any illusion.

As a result of this question, this inquiry, this introspection, such a unique awakening and consciousness comes that you feel you have been shaken out of a sleep. Then you begin to see that the castles you built have been built in a dream, that the boats in which you have been sailing were made of paper. Your whole life begins to seem unreal, as if it were not yours but someone else's. It actually is not yours, it is part of some drama you have been acting out – a drama which education, training, culture, tradition and society have taught you, but the roots of which are not in you.

If the flowers arranged in a vase were to become conscious in some way, they will know that they have no roots; the same is bound to happen to you if you become conscious. We are not really men. We are mere deceptions, without any roots, without any ground. We are like characters in a fairy tale, in a dream, with no existence in reality. I see you lost and moving in this dream. All your actions are done in sleep. All your activities take place in sleep. But you can awaken from this sleep. This is the difference between sleep and death. You can awaken from the former, but not from the latter. No matter how deep your sleep, awakening is its intrinsic possibility. Sleep has this dormant seed, this potentiality hidden within it.

If you come face-to-face with yourself many illusions will be shattered, as if somebody falsely considering himself very beautiful finds himself before a mirror for the very first time. Just as there is a mirror for looking at the body, there is a mirror for looking at the self. I am talking about this very mirror. Self-observation is this mirror.

Do you really want to see the truth of yourself? Do you want to meet the person that is really you? And knowing there is the possibility of seeing yourself in all your nakedness, don't you feel afraid? Such fear is quite natural. It is because of this fear that we go on creating new dreams about ourselves and keeping our true reality forgotten. But these dreams cannot be your companions; you cannot get anywhere with their help. They only waste the time and the priceless opportunity that could have led you home.

You must wonder why I insist so much on your seeing the nakedness, the ugliness and the emptiness of yourselves. Wouldn't it be better to leave what is unfit to be seen, unseen? And isn't it nice, isn't it good to decorate what is ugly with jewelry and to cover what isn't worth seeing with curtains? Generally this is exactly what we do. This is the common custom. This is in vogue. But this is very harmful because the wounds we hide do not heal. On the contrary they become all the more infected and dangerous. And the ugliness we cover up is not destroyed but enters the inner source of our whole personality. We go on sprinkling artificial perfume on the surface while a foul stink rules inside. A time comes when perfume no longer helps and the inner stink begins to surface on the outside, when jewelry no longer helps and the underlying ugliness forces its way out.

I am not in favor of sprinkling perfume; I am in favor of

getting rid of foul smells. I am not for covering ugliness with jewelry and flowers; I am for doing away with ugliness from the roots and awakening the beauty and music within. In their absence everything else is pointless. All our efforts are useless. All our endeavors are like trying to get oil by pressing sand.

So I ask you to uncover what is hidden in yourself. Uncover yourself and know yourself. Do not run away from yourself. And escaping from yourself is not possible. Where will you go? What you are will be with you wherever you go. You can transform it but you cannot run away from it.

Self-observation is the first link in this chain of transformation. And the wonder of wonders is that to know the ugliness is to become free of it! To know one's fear is to become free of that fear; to know hatred is to become free of hatred. They are there because we do not look at them. They are after us because we are trying to run away from them. The moment we stop they will also stop – just as our shadow runs with us when we are running and stops when we stop.

If we can look at these things the whole scenario is immediately transformed. What we thought were ghosts and spirits were merely our shadows. Because we were running, these ghosts and spirits ran after us – and they made us run even more! The moment we stop running they become lifeless; the moment we look at them they cease to exist. They are just shadows, and surely shadows can't do anything. There was the shadow of ugliness, so to cover it we clothed and decorated it with flowers – and thus we created an illusion. Now, when we see it was just a shadow and clothing, it becomes unnecessary; we become free of the shadow and aware of that to whom the shadow belongs. This very awareness gives birth to the vision of the beautiful one, the supremely beautiful one.

I have had this vision; I stopped running away from shadows and that gave me the strength to look beyond them. And what I saw there – that truth – transformed everything. Truth transforms everything. Its very presence is the revolution. Hence I say to you don't be afraid. Look at what really is and don't take shelter in dreams and imaginations. He who dares to give up these shelters is sheltered by truth.

This morning someone asked me what does it mean to know oneself directly. To know yourself directly means not to accept other people's opinions about you. See for yourself what is there within you – what is hidden in your thoughts, in your passions, in your actions, in your desires and longings. Look at these things directly, just as you look at a completely new place after arriving there. Look at yourself as one looks at an unfamiliar person, at a stranger. This will do you a lot of good. The greatest good will be that the grand image you have created of yourself in your mind will shatter to pieces. This shattering of the idol is a must, because it is only after this imaginary idol has been destroyed that you pass from the land of dreams into the land of reality.

Before we can become the truth and the good, we must first shatter our illusions of being the truth and the good which we have invented to hide the untruth and evil in ourselves. These illusions were self-deceptions. Nobody creates a fictitious image and personality for himself for nothing. This too is done out of some necessity. It is done in order to save oneself from humiliation in one's own eyes. When one glimpses the animal that resides in him, the very presence of the animal torments him and he feels humiliated in himself.

There are two ways to save yourself from this humiliation: either the animal has to disappear or you just have to forget about it. In order for it to disappear you must pass through a spiritual discipline. But it is very easy to forget the animal. It is a very simple thing. Imagination alone is enough for that. We create an imaginary image of ourselves for our eyes alone, and with the help of this image the animal is suppressed. But it does not disappear. It remains active behind this image. In fact, this image is only an outward appearance; at the back of it lies the animal. Don't you see this image losing out, being defeated every day in real life, in real situations? This is only natural. The animal inside is the reality and so it defeats all our efforts. Every day the imaginary personality is defeated by it.

Yet despite this, you keep your images alive and adorned. And all the time you are busy trying to find ways to prove to others and to yourselves that they are real – through your charities, through your sacrifices, through your acts of mercy and service. Aren't all of these so-called moral actions just a search for evidence? But all of this is to no avail. The image you have constructed of yourself remains dead, it remains lifeless; there is no possibility that life can enter it.

I ask you to free yourselves from this dead weight. Let this false, dead companion go, and know and understand the one who is real. The path is not through the former but through the latter, and it is in order to avoid this latter path that you have created all your self-deceptions.

Last night I passed a field where I saw scarecrows. Sticks had been put up and dressed in shirts. On the top, as heads, were earthen pots. In the darkness the birds and the animals take them to be watchmen and are frightened away. I looked at the scarecrows and also at the people who were with me. Then I said, "Let us look within ourselves to see if we too aren't scarecrows." At this my companions began to laugh. But I saw that their laughter was completely false.

Everything about us has become false – our whole lives, our behavior, our laughter, our tears, everything has become false. We become exhausted carrying the weight of this falsehood. And although this falsehood is heavy, we don't throw it off because we are even more afraid of what lies behind it. We are afraid to go in there, for the one we always thought of as ourselves is nowhere to be found. And the one whose presence we have always scorned in others is there in its full intensity. Our fear does not allow us to uncover our selves.

For the life of spiritual endeavor, meditation, fearlessness is the first condition. He who cannot dare this, cannot enter within himself. Far greater courage is needed to go into oneself than the courage required to walk along a wild, lonely, unknown path on a dark night, because as soon as a man enters himself all the sweet dreams he has cherished for so long about himself are shattered and he finds himself face to face with the ugliest and most sordid of sins – sins from which he thought he was totally free.

But he who courageously uncovers himself and moves into the dark lanes and valleys within himself, into places long abandoned, finds that he has embarked upon a new life. With this daring plunge into the darkness he embarks on a journey which ultimately leads to the attainment of light. He has been seeking it for many lives, but it has always eluded him because he dared not walk into the darkness.

Darkness has enveloped and hidden the light just like a heap of ashes hides a spark of fire. As soon as we penetrate the darkness the light is seen. That is why I say to you: if you want light, do not be afraid of the darkness. The man who is afraid of darkness will never find the light. The path to light passes through darkness. As a matter of fact, this daring to enter the darkness is itself transformed into the light within. It is through this daring that what has been so far asleep, awakes.

I see that you are desirous of attaining self-knowledge but are afraid of knowing yourself as you really are. Statements such as "the soul is truth, consciousness, bliss" or "it is eternally pure buddha nature" please you. But that is because they help you forget what you really are – the complete antithesis of truth, consciousness, bliss – and help you nourish your ego.

That is why sinners crowd around your so-called saints and monks. The talk they hear there is about the purity of the soul and about being one with *brahman* and it's all very pleasing to them. This way their self reproach, their self-pity is reduced, their sense of inferiority is suppressed and they are once again able to stand tall in their own eyes. This has only one outcome: it goes on becoming easier for them to commit sin, since the soul is pure and is not affected by it! Believing that your soul is eternally pure and is the buddha nature does not put an end to sin. It is only a very deep self-deception. It is the last trick of the human mind. By merely believing there is no darkness you do not have light.

An ideology that teaches you to believe that sin does not exist and that the soul is not involved in sin is very deceptive. It is just a means of forgetting your sinful condition. It does not lead to the elimination of sin, but to forgetfulness of sin, which is even worse than the existence of sin. To be able to see your sins, to be aware of them is good, beneficial. Not to see your sins, to be unconscious of them is harmful, because when they are seen they begin to goad us, they begin to prick at us, they begin to inspire us to transform ourselves. Awareness of sin brings about change, and a total awareness of sin causes instantaneous revolution, transformation.

So, please don't get involved in talk such as "the eternally pure buddha nature of the soul" and so on. This is not something to do with belief. It is a direct realization experienced when the sin-ridden personality has been cast off and the seeker, breaking through the layers of darkness, enters his own secret, innermost center of light. It is a direct realization. It is not something to be conceptualized.

Any imaginary concept of it is going to be very harmful. It can become a hindrance on the way to light, because if you believe there is no darkness, there is no question of your trying to remove something that does not exist. And if the soul commits neither good nor evil, then what is the point of rising above them? These hollow statements of the so-called metaphysicists have kept many people in unawareness. This poison has spread too far and because of it, although we think of ourselves as gods it would be difficult to find greater sinners than us on earth!

Don't forget that all this talk about the purity of the soul and its impact is really directed toward remaining oblivious to sin. It becomes very difficult for those who fall into the trap of this talk to get out of it later. It is easy to become free from sin but it is very difficult to escape the clutches of this dangerous kind of metaphysics.

The fact that the soul is pure is not a theory nor a principle, it is a direct realization. And any discussion about it is useless. It is like creating an illusion in the mind of a sick man that his sickness does not exist. If the sick man accepts this as gospel, the result won't be recovery but only death.

Those who know do not discuss realization. They talk about the spiritual practice, the meditation that leads to realization. What deserves consideration is not the realization but the spiritual discipline. Realization is bound to follow the discipline. It is useless to think about it. And if anyone takes realization as a belief, then any discipline will be impossible for him.

And how easy and pleasant it is to believe in realization without spiritual discipline or practice! This way one begins to enjoy freedom from sin without actually being rid of it, and in a deep mist of deception beggars begin to enjoy being emperors. What a joy it must be for beggars to be told that they are emperors and not beggars! It is no wonder that those who tell them so are very much respected and are worshipped at their feet. There cannot be an easier and cheaper liberation from self-poverty and sin! This hollow metaphysics, this pseudo philosophy gives them a very easy liberation, whereas spiritual discipline, meditation, requires great effort on their part.

I hope you are not caught in the trap of any such metaphysics or metaphysician. I hope you have not resorted to any such short cut. The easiest and cheapest way is just to believe that the soul is eternally pure and enlightened, that the soul is *brahman* itself and hence there is nothing to be done by you. In other words, everything that you happen to be doing at the time is all right because there is nothing worth giving up.

Remember that even truth can be abused, and even the most noble truths can be used to hide the meanest lies. This has happened in the past and it happens every day. Cowardice can be hidden under the guise of nonviolence, sin can be hidden under the philosophy of the eternally pure and enlightened state of the soul, and lethargy under the garb of sannyas.

I want to warn you against these deceptions. He who is not alert about them cannot make much progress in himself. Don't seek shelter in any philosophical jargon in order to escape from the sin and darkness that have enshrouded you. Know them. Become familiar with them. They are there. Don't try to forget their existence. Even though they are like dreams, they are still there. And don't think that dreams don't exist. Even a dream has its own existence. It can also overwhelm us, affect us. Saying and believing "It was just a dream" leads nowhere. There is no other way than waking up from it. But if one likes, he can even dream he has woken up. A hollow metaphysics, a metaphysics void of meditation does this very thing. It does not awaken you, it simply gives you a dream of awakening. This is a dream within a dream. Haven't you had dreams where you have seen yourself as awake?

Merely believing and saying that there is no sin, no darkness, serves no purpose. It is only an expression of your desire, not of the truth. It is your desire that there should be no sin, no darkness, but desiring alone is not enough. Desire alone is impotent. And gradually these metaphysicians begin to believe the dreams of attainment, just as a beggar desiring all the time to be a king will ultimately start dreaming he has become one. Always wishing for it, they finally imagine they have attained it, although in actuality they have not achieved anything. This way it becomes easy to forget defeat. Having achieved in a dream what they could not in reality, they have a sigh of satisfaction.

I hope you are not seeking such satisfaction here. If so, you have come to the wrong person. I cannot give you any dreams. I cannot give you any basis for self-deception. I am a dream-breaker and I want to wake you from your slumber. If this creates pain, please forgive me for that.

Awakening is painful, without a doubt, but this pain is the only penance. This penance, this pain, begins with your awareness of your actual sinful condition, awareness of the reality of the sorry state of yourself. You are not to cling to any illusions; you are to know what is as it is. This will cause unhappiness and this will cause pain because it will destroy the sweet dreams in which you see yourselves as emperors. The emperor will disappear and the beggar will stand in the light; beauty will vanish and ugliness will appear; good will evaporate and evil will become visible; the animal in you will stand before you in all his nakedness.

This is all necessary, very necessary. It is essential to pass through this agony. It is inevitable because it is the labor of childbirth. And it is only after this, after we have seen this animal face to face, that we will begin to know clearly the one who is not the animal.

A man who sees the animal face to face becomes different and separate from the animal. This awakening to the animal within breaks the identification with it. The observation separates the observer from the observed and that seed is sown within us, which when fully developed flowers into self-realization.

So, running away from sin, from darkness and from the animal is not a spiritual discipline but an escape from it. It is like the ostrich hiding its head in the sand and feeling secure in the thought that since it cannot see the enemy, the enemy does not exist. How nice it would be if this were true! But it isn't. The enemy not being visible doesn't mean he does not exist. On the contrary, he becomes more dangerous that way. You will be an easier prey with your eyes closed. In the presence of an enemy your eyes should be open all the wider, since knowledge of the enemy is in your interest.

Ignorance can do us nothing but harm. It is for this reason I ask you to uncover your dark side fully and to observe it. Take off all your clothes and see what you are. Set aside all your doctrines and theories and see what you are. Lift your head out of the sand and look.

The very opening of your eyes – this very looking – is a transformation, the beginning of a new life. With the opening of your eyes a transformation begins, and whatsoever you do after that takes you to the truth. Breaking through the layers of darkness, you walk into the light; sweeping away the webs of sin, you move into the divine; destroying ignorance, you attain to the soul.

This is the right path for self-realization. And before this no dreams need be dreamed – no dreams about the soul and God, no dreams about *brahman* as truth, consciousness, bliss. Those are the ways of denying facts under the same logic as that of the ostrich. That is not the path of right action, rather a false satisfaction of the lethargic.

Last night someone asked me, "What is *satsang*?" I told him, "*Satsang* means being in the company of one's own self. The truth is not to be found outside. No teacher, no scripture can give it to you. It is inside you and if you wish to attain it, seek your own company. Be with yourself." But we are always in the company of everyone and anyone except our own.

Eckehart was once sitting all alone under a grove of trees in a lonely place. A friend who was passing by saw him sitting there. He went up to him and said, "I saw you sitting, lonely, and I thought I would keep you company and so I have come over to join you." Do you know what Eckehart replied? He said, "I was with myself, but you have come, and if anything I am feeling lonely now."

Are you ever in your own company like this? This is *satsang*.

This is prayerfulness. This is meditation. When you are all alone within yourself and there is no thought, no thought of anyone, you are in the company of your self. When the outer world is absent inside, there is the company of your self. In that companionlessness and solitude, in that absolute aloneness, the truth is realized because in your innermost being you yourself are that truth.

It is a question of *being* religious, not of appearing religious. Whenever anyone asks me about being religious the first thing I inquire of him is, "Do you want to appear religious or to become religious?" The two are quite different dimensions. Being religious involves a discipline for self-realization; appearing religious is just self-adornment. The garbs of the hermits and monks, their stereotyped, conventional robes, their looks, the decorative marks on their foreheads and bodies, and other paraphernalia – all these are for appearing religious. If you too want to appear religious like this, it is very easy.

But remember, appearing is for others, being is for oneself. I am not what others know of me from the outside. I am what I know myself to be from the inside. If I appear healthy to you, does it hold any value in it? The value is only in my actually being healthy.

Like religious clothes, religious qualities can also be worn. People wear them like ornaments of decoration. And this deception is even deeper. Man's behavior can be of two kinds, like that of real flowers or like that of plastic flowers. The first come from the very life and being of the plant; the others have no life in them at all. They don't bloom into flowers, instead they have to be put together. Authentic behavior blooms, false behavior is put together from the outside. Man's behavior is very symbolic. It represents his interiority. What is meaningful is to change the interiority, not the behavior.

When we have a fever and the body is running a temperature, we don't try to get rid of the fever by bringing down the temperature. We try to reduce the fever and this brings the temperature down. Temperature is only a symptom of the fever, not a disease in itself. It is only an indication, it is not an enemy. What would you call those who begin to battle with temperature itself?

This same kind of nonsense goes on concerning religious life, moral life. Outward indications are mistaken for the enemy, the symptoms are taken for the disease, and we begin to fight with them. This does not help to eliminate the disease, on the contrary it is the patient who will surely be eliminated.

Ego, untruth, violence, lust, anger, greed, infatuation are all indications, symptoms. They are the temperature, not the disease. They are not to be fought against directly; through them we need only to know there is an enemy within. Ignorance of the self is this enemy. It is this ignorance of the self that is expressed in a variety of ways, like ego, untruth, violence, lust, fear and anger. Hence, destroying these cannot destroy the ignorance of the self, because that is the root and these are merely its expressions.

Anyway, these symptoms cannot be destroyed directly. At the most you end up putting plastic flowers of truth over untruth, of nonviolence over violence and of fearlessness over fear. You may have decorated yourselves with such flowers, and they may have deceived others, but I hope you are not deceived by them yourself.

The question is not that of getting rid of untruth, violence and fear, but of getting rid of the ignorance of the self. That alone is the problem. They are all there because of this ignorance. Without it they have no existence. If there is no ignorance of the self, all these disappear automatically and in their place arise truth, non-ego, desirelessness, non-anger, nonviolence, nonpossessiveness. They too are symptoms. They are the symptoms of self-realization.

CHAPTER 9

The Fully Drowned

I am unable to give you the truth. If anyone says he is capable of giving it to you, you can be certain he is giving you an untruth from the very beginning. No one is capable to give the truth. This is no comment on the capacity of the giver, it only shows that truth is a living thing. It is not a material object that can be given or taken. It is a living experience and an experience one must obtain by oneself.

Dead objects can be given or taken, not experiences. Can I transfer to you the love, the experience of love that I have had? Can I give you the experience of beauty and the music that I have had? How I wish I could hand over the bliss which has happened in such an extraordinary way to this ordinary looking body of mine! But there is no way to do so. I am in pain wishing to share this, but there is no way. This is such helplessness.

A friend of mine was born blind. How I wished I could transfer my sight to him, but it wasn't possible. Perhaps one day it may become possible because eyes are parts of the body and may be capable of being transplanted. But the sight that sees the truth can never be transferred, no matter how strongly one might wish it. It belongs to the realm of the soul, not to the realm of the body.

Whatever is attained in the world of the soul is only attained directly for oneself. In the world of the soul, no borrowing, no dependence on others is possible. Nobody can walk there on borrowed legs. There is no other refuge there except in oneself. To attain to truth one must be one's own refuge. This is the inescapable condition.

This is why I said I am incapable of giving you the truth. Only words are passed on in the transfer, words that are lifeless and dead – the truth is always left behind. And the communication of words alone is not really a communication at all. That which is alive in them – that meaning, that experience which is their life – does not go with them. They are like empty cartridges. They are like dead bodies, corpses. They can only be a burden to you; they can never liberate you. In words you only receive the corpse of truth, there is no heartbeat of truth in it.

As I said, truth cannot be given. But I can be of some assistance in helping you set down this load that has been put on you and made heavier and heavier over the centuries. It is a must to be free from this burden of words. Just as dust covers a traveler while he is walking along the road, the dust of words and thoughts gathers on one during the journey through life. This is only natural. But it is necessary to brush this dust off.

Words are dead things; they are not the truth. Nobody's words are the truth. Do not collect them. Collecting them is harmful. The pilgrimage to truth cannot be made carrying this crushing weight. Just as a climber must lay down his pack before scaling a mountain to seek the heights, one who has embarked on the journey to truth had better lay down the burden of words. A consciousness free of words becomes capable of attaining the lofty heights of truth.

I teach only one kind of non-possessiveness, the non-possession of words and thoughts. Their dead weight is making your journey very arduous. Chuang Tzu has said, "The net is for catching fish. Please, catch the fish and throw away the net." But we are such bad fishermen that we catch hold of the nets and forget about the fish. Look at the tops of your heads. You are carrying the boats on top of your heads and you are forgetting that you are to sail in them.

Words are indications. They are signposts, they themselves are not the truth. Understand their indication and then throw them away. Collecting signs is no different from collecting corpses.

Words are like fingers pointing to the moon. He who concentrates his attention on the fingers misses the moon. The fingers serve their purpose if they lead you away from themselves. But if, on the contrary, they draw you and entangle you in themselves, then they have become not only useless but truly harmful.

Haven't the words you have learned about truth become a source of misfortune to you already? Haven't they separated you from one another, haven't they separated man from man? Aren't all the stupidities and cruelties perpetrated in the name of religion because of words? Aren't all those sects which are known as the various religions just based on the differences of words?

Truth is one and can only be one, but words are many – just like the moon is one, but the fingers pointing to her may be a thousand and one. Those who have held on to one or other of the countless words that are pointing to the truth are responsible for the many religious sects. These religions have not arisen from truth but from words. Truth is one. Religion too is one. Those who are capable of letting go of words attain to this non-dual religion and to this non-dual truth.

So, I don't want to add to your burden of words with more words. You are already breaking down under this heavy load of words. I can feel very well that your heads are bent under their weight.

Those who have known the truth do not open their mouths at all. Their lips are sealed. Not a word is to be heard from them about truth. Aren't they saying enough through this? Aren't they saying that truth resides in silence, that silence itself is truth? But we fail to understand this. We cannot understand anything without words. Our understanding is limited to words and so they speak to us through the medium of words. They tell us in words about that which cannot be communicated in words. It is their compassion that leads them to attempt this impossible feat, and it is our ignorance that catches hold of those words. Words coupled with ignorance make a sect, words plus ignorance is a sect – and in this way we remain deprived yet once again of the truth, and religion remains as distant from us as it ever has been.

You must rise above words. Only then will you experience what is behind the words. Words only fill your memory, knowing does not come from them. And please don't mistake memory for knowing. Memory is nothing more than a record of the past. It is learning, not knowing.

Someone asked Ramana Maharshi what he should do to know the truth. He replied, "Forget everything that you know." If only you could forget all you know! Out of this forgetting would emerge the innocence and simplicity in which the truth and the self are known.

When words and thoughts formed out of words do not crowd your consciousness, light finds a way in. In that free moment you are in contact with knowing. You have to open the windows and doors of consciousness. In fact, all the walls now surrounding the consciousness have to be pulled down. Then you will meet the light that is your true nature. Certainly in order to meet the sky one has to become like the sky – empty, free, boundless. Thoughts do not allow this to happen, they surround you like clouds. These clouds must be dispersed. Then how could I spread more clouds of thought over your mind?

What I am telling you, or what I want to tell you but am unable to do, is not a thought, a belief or an idea as such – it is an experience, a direct realization. Were it simply a thought, it would have been possible to communicate – and even had the experience been of the outer world, some word or other would have communicated it. But this experience is not of the outer world. It is the experience of the one who experiences everything. It is the knowing of the knower. And there lies the difficulty.

Usually in knowledge, the knower and the known are separate, the seer and the seen are distinct, but in the realization of the self they are not separate. Here, the knower, the known and the knowing are all one. And so here, words become quite useless. They are not created to be used in this context. To use them in this area is to stretch them beyond their capacity, beyond their potential. No wonder they become completely crippled and lifeless in this tug-of-war. And although they give an indication of the body, of the outer form of truth, they cannot touch the soul of truth.

How can words express the truth which can only be known when words are not present? That which is attained in a state of thoughtlessness cannot be tied down by thoughts. Is there a way to tie down the sky? And can we call it the sky if it can be tied down? Why don't we think of truth in the same way? Is truth any less boundless or infinite than the sky?

If the sky were packed in bundles and put on sale in the market nobody would come forward to buy it. But we do this about truth: truth, God and liberation are all on sale in the market. And the vendors are not to blame. They are only supplying the demands of the buyers. And as long as there are buyers, as long as there are customers for truth, it won't be possible to do away with the shops that offer ready-made truth. All the organizations and all the sects operating in the name of religion have turned into shops. You buy ready-made truth in them. Not only are ready-made clothes available in the market, ready-made truth is also for sale there. I cannot give you ready-made truth. Ready-made truth simply does not exist.

I remember a story:

A master once asked his disciple a question about truth. The latter replied and the master said, "Yes, that is right."

The next day the master asked the same question. The disciple said, "I already replied to it yesterday."

The master said, "Answer again today."

The disciple repeated what he had said the previous day, whereupon the master said, "No! No!"

The disciple was surprised and said to his master, "Yesterday you said, 'Yes, that is right,' so how is it that you say no today?"

Do you know what the master answered? He said, "Yesterday it was yes, today it is no."

What is the point of this story? Do you get it? The point is that the disciple's answer had become stereotyped, it was imprisoned in a fixed pattern. It was confined to a concept. Hence it had lost its life; it was dead. It had become a part of the memory. It was no more a knowing. Our memories are full of such dead answers and because of that, that which is alive cannot arise.

My friends, you have to awaken experience – experiencing – not memory. Memory is a dead weight; experiencing is a living liberation. The experience of truth cannot be predetermined. It cannot be imprisoned in any terminology or in any rigid definition perpetrated by some philosophy, religion or ideology. We cannot expect the truth to conform to any ideology or to any school of thought or to any set rules. Any effort to confine it to any pattern will be futile.

It is not that we have to confine or imprison truth, but on the contrary, we have to unravel ourselves, liberate ourselves. The way to truth is not to confine it, the way is to unravel ourselves. Do not imprison truth; unravel yourself. This is the only way to attain to it. The realization of truth is only possible through experiencing. It cannot be known by any other means than self-realization or self-experience. Experiencing and experiencing alone is the deciding factor.

Once I was by a waterfall. I drank its water and found it to be sweet. This also applies to truth. Drink and know. It is the kind of taste you can only know by tasting it.

Truth is not a product of your knowledge. It is not your creation. You do not manufacture it. Nobody does, nobody can. It is already there. Hence it can't be had anywhere ready-made, it is already there. The moment you open your eyes it is seen; the moment you shut them it is not seen. It is just like light. You don't have to buy it. You just have to open your eyes and then the truth emerges in its total originality, in its perfect purity, in the wholeness of its existence – and it transforms you. For this to be possible it is essential that you do not corrupt yourself with borrowed thoughts or accept the leftovers of others. Don't you know that life does not accept anything stale or dead?

What then shall I say to you? I shall not speak about truth. Then what shall I speak about? I shall speak to you about how truth can be known. I shall not speak to you about light, but will tell you how you can open your eyes and see the light. I won't say what I am seeing, but I will say how I am seeing it. That alone can be told. And it is a blessing that at least this much can be said.

Religion, true religion, has nothing to do with the *doctrine* of truth, rather it has to do with the *method* of knowing truth. Hence I shall not say anything about truth. I don't want to make you feel you know it before you actually know it. I wish to take you to the place where you can know it for yourself, to the point where you can have a look at it, to that boiling point where your ignorance will evaporate and you will meet the smokeless, pure flame that you yourself are.

Now let us talk about that method.

Those who aspire to walk along the path to truth find two doors open to them: one of them is of thinking about truth; the other, of spiritual endeavor for the attainment of truth. One is the path of reasoning; the other, of meditation. One is the way of contemplation of the truth; the other, of discipline leading to its attainment. There seem to be these two doors. But as I see it, the door is only one. The other one does not exist, it simply appears to. This other door is just an illusion.

The door of thinking about truth is not a real door. It is a false and illusory door and many get lost there. Through the door of thought, by thinking about truth, you never get anywhere. In spite of much traveling you find yourself standing where you began. It has only a beginning, it does not have an end. And something that does not have an end can only be an illusion at its beginning.

Thinking about the truth, what will you do? How will you think about the truth? You cannot think about something that is not known. How will a thought think about the unknown? Its reach is only within the realm of the known. Thinking can supply questions, it cannot supply solutions. Anyone who solely pursues thinking may find himself lost in chaos; his mind may end up in a kind of madness. That many a thinker goes crazy is not accidental and not without reason. This is the ultimate conclusion of thinking, its ultimate outcome. The way of thinking is not a way to attain to truth at all.

Let me tell you a story, a wonderful story:

Once upon a time a man set out in search of the end of the world. After a long journey, after an almost endless pilgrimage he arrived at a temple where the words "This is the end of the world" were written. He was very surprised but couldn't believe what he saw written there. It was unbelievable. He continued on and within a short time reached the place where the world came to an end. A deep abyss and a void was in front of him. He looked down into it. There was absolutely nothing there. His breath almost stopped and his head began to reel. He turned and ran. And never again did he turn to look back.

This is a story about the end of thinking. If we think about the truth we will continue thinking and thinking and thinking and we will reach a point where further thinking becomes impossible. This is the end of thinking. There will be an abyss in front of us and our minds will refuse to take one more step.

Such a moment comes in the process of thinking if we carry it through to the end. It is inevitable. And if you still feel there is something more to think about, know that you have not yet truly reached the end. When there is nothing more to think about, absolutely nothing, and not a single step forward is possible, know that the end is real and that you have arrived at the temple where the world ends.

If that man who reached the end of the world had asked me what to do, I would not have advised him to run away. Can you imagine what advice I would have given him? I would have told him that since he had journeyed so far it would be better to take just one more step, the last and the most important one. I would have asked him to jump boldly into the abyss, the void that lay in front of him. I would have told him that only this one more step was necessary and to keep in mind that where the world ends the kingdom of God begins.

The point where the world ends is also the point where the realm of the divine begins and there is no point more important than that. Where thinking ends, seeing begins. Where thinking ends, truth is realized. You have to jump from thought into thoughtlessness. From words you must jump into nothingness, into emptiness. This is the method. This is courage. This is true asceticism. This is true spiritual seeking.

If at this point you see a vision of Brahma, Vishnu and Mahesh, know that you are still thinking. If you see Mahavira, Buddha or Krishna, be aware that you are still dreaming dreams. Then you have not reached the real end. The real end is where there is nothing to be thought of, nothing to be seen, nothing to be known. Only you and the emptiness remain. In fact, you are not there either. Only the void, nothingness, is there.

You are standing at the end of the world. Your mind will want to go back. It will want to do so with all its might. This is the moment when courage is needed and you have to take one more step. Just one more step, a jump, is expected of you – and everything is transformed. Then there is no more thinking, only seeing, realization. Then you have known. You know when you drop all knowing; you see when you give up all seeking. And when you cease to be in every way, then for the first time you really are. The discipline of self-realization is a jump into the valley of death. But that is the only way to realize immortality. The method is not thinking, but a jump out of thinking. The jump out of thinking is meditation.

Every day I am talking of this very thing. Thoughts are the waves on the ocean of consciousness. They are like transient bubbles, disappearing almost before they are formed. They indicate a troubled and agitated surface. One who is in them cannot be in any depth. To be in them is to be in shallow water. All thoughts are shallow. No thought can be deep, because no wave can be in the depths. Waves are possible only on the surface. Thoughts too are just the play on the surface of consciousness. The ocean is not in the waves, the waves are in the ocean. There cannot be waves without an ocean, but there can be an ocean without waves. There cannot be any thoughts without consciousness, but there can be consciousness without thoughts.

Consciousness is the source, the basis. If you wish to know it you will have to move behind the waves, you will have to go beyond the waves. You are not to keep sitting on the seashore. Kabir has said, "I went in search, but foolishly kept sitting on the shore." Please don't sit on the shore in this same way. There is nothing on the shore, you are to move into that to which the shore belongs. The shore is only there so you can jump into the sea.

And it is also possible that a man may not remain standing on the shore but may remain floating on the waves. In my view, that too is only the shore. Whatever stops one from diving in and drowning is the shore. People swimming in thought are like this. They are under the illusion that they have left the shore but in actual fact they haven't.

When Mahavira died, he left a guidance for his beloved disciple Gautama who was absent at the time. He said, "Tell Gautama that he has crossed the river quite nicely, but why is he now holding fast to the shore? Let go of that too." To what shore was Mahavira referring? I am also speaking of the same shore. It is the shore of thinking; it is the shore of swimming in thoughts.

Truth is attained by diving, not by swimming. Swimming takes place on the surface; diving takes you to the endless depths. You have to plunge from the shore of thoughts into the depths of the void. There is a lovely couplet from the poet Bihari: "Those undrowned really drowned; those fully drowned crossed."

What are your intentions then? If you want to cross, then the courage to drown yourself is an absolute necessity. I teach you that very drowning, that very disappearance so that you can cross the ocean, so that you can be what you really are.

CHAPTER 10

Entering the Gap

Osho,
According to you, nobody is able to impart the truth. Is what you say not true then?

What I am telling you is only an indication and should not be regarded as the truth itself. It is not the indicator you have to see, but where it points to. While you are looking there what you will see is the truth. There is no way to speak that truth. No sooner has it been uttered than it becomes false. The truth becomes the experience but never the expression.

Osho,
You suggest that we fully drown. How can we do this?

I tell you from my own experience that there is nothing easier and simpler than drowning – drowning in one's own self. The only thing one has to do for this is not to seek the support of anything on the surface the mind. By catching hold of thoughts one is unable to drown, and because of their support one remains on the surface.

We are in the habit of catching hold of thoughts. As soon as one thought passes on we catch hold of another – but we never enter the gap between two successive thoughts. This gap itself is the door to drowning into the depths. Do not move into thoughts, move into that which is between them.

How can this be done? It can be done by waking up to the thoughts. Just as a man standing on the side of a road watches the people passing by, you should observe your thoughts. They are simply pedestrians, passing by on the road of the mind within you. Just watch them. Don't choose any of them this way or that. Don't form judgments about any of them. If you can observe them with detachment and indifference, your "fist" that has been gripping them opens automatically and you find yourself standing, not in thoughts, but in the interval, in the gap between them. But the gap has no foundation so it isn't possible just to stand there. Simply by being there you drown.

And this drowning itself is to find the real support, because it is through this that you reach the reality you truly are. One who seeks support in the realm of thoughts is really suspended in the air without support, but he who throws away all crutches attains the support of his own self.

Osho,
I want to conquer my mind but it seems to be an impossibility. Yet you say it is a very easy matter. What do you mean?

In the very idea of conquest I see the seed of the impossibility of conquest. And it is this very mistake that does not allow man to conquer. If you want to conquer your own shadow will you be able to? As soon as you know the shadow to be a shadow you have won it over. The shadow isn't to be conquered, it is just to be known. And what is true of the shadow is also true of the mind. I ask you to know the mind, not to conquer it.

Someone once reverently asked Bodhidharma, "My mind is very restless. Will you please show me the way to calm it?" Bodhidharma posed a question in reply: "Where is your mind? Bring it to me and I will calm it." The man said, "That is the difficulty. It eludes all my attempts to catch it."

If I had been in Bodhidharma's place I would have then said, "Do not try to catch it, let it go. Your very desire to catch it is its restlessness. Can you ever catch a shadow?"

Do you know what else Bodhidharma said then? He said, "Look, I have calmed it, have I not?"

If you can only watch your mind and not try to catch it or to conquer it, it will no more be found. In the old days when they were trying to saddle-break a horse, they used to ask whether it was better to tire the horse out or to strengthen the reins. These were also the two methods for conquering the mind, for bringing it under control. But I don't prescribe either of the two methods. I ask you to first look if there really is a horse at all. You are out to exhaust, harness and saddle something that does not exist at all. Both efforts are false because there is no horse. The horse is the shadow of your unawareness. If you wake up, there is neither a horse nor a mind to conquer or bring under control.

Osho,
You ask us not to hold on to thoughts. Does this apply to good thoughts as well?

If you want to know your real self you must rid yourself of both good and evil and become empty, without content. Good thoughts, bad thoughts, both are acquired things. They have come from outside: they are both things taken in. Your real self-nature is hidden under them, behind their cover. Thoughts as such are a covering. They are like chains keeping you bound.

It is necessary to break these chains. It makes no difference whether the chains are of iron or of gold.

Whatsoever has come from without is an acquired thing, an accumulation. Non-accumulation means that state of pure consciousness where no outside impressions exist. The revelation of the soul becomes possible only in the absence of all conditionings. And for that, the foundation of an unconditioned mind is a must. But we are full of thoughts. And those who are religious are even more full of religious thoughts. This is what is understood by "being religious"! Being full of the scriptures is considered being religious. This is absolutely wrong.

A master once said to one of his learned disciples, "Everything else is fine, but there is still one defect in you." The disciple thought about it for many days but was unable to find any defect in his conduct and behavior so he asked the master about it. The master replied, "You have altogether too much religion in you. You are too full of it. This is the only defect that remains in you, but this is no ordinary defect."

How can there be *too* much religion? Yes, there can be too many religious scriptures, too much religious thought stuffed in the mind. This makes your mind so burdened that it cannot fly away into the sky of truth.

That is why I ask you to become empty. Rid yourself completely of all thoughts, of all impressions and then see what happens in that emptiness. The greatest miracle of life takes place in that emptiness, in that void. That void brings you face-to-face with yourself. There is no greater miracle than this because as soon as you stand face-to-face with yourself you become face-to-face with God.

Osho,
I am an idol-worshipper, but according to your ideas it seems there is no need for an idol. Should I give up idol-worship?

I do not ask you to give up anything or to take on anything. I am simply calling you to wake up. If when you wake up, your dreams are over, it will be another story. Behavior changes along with levels of consciousness. When children grow up they automatically stop playing with dolls. They don't make any effort to give it up, it stops automatically.

There once lived a mystic on the outskirts of a village. He lived alone in a hut without doors. There was nothing in the hut that made doors necessary. One day some soldiers happened by. They went into the hut and asked for water. One of them asked the mystic why, since he was a religious man, there wasn't a single idol of God anywhere in the hut. The mystic replied, "This hut is very small. Where is the room for two here?"

The soldiers were amused at the mystic's words, and the next day they brought him a statue of God as a gift. But the mystic said, "I don't need any image of God because he himself has been living here for a long time. I have disappeared. Don't you see there isn't room for two here?" The soldiers saw he was pointing to his heart. That was his hut.

God is formless. Energy can only be formless; it can have no shape. Consciousness cannot have shape. It is boundless. The whole, the totality can have no boundaries. It is beginningless and endless because "that which is" cannot even have a beginning and an end.

How childish we are that we create idols of one with no beginning and no end. And then we worship these self-created idols. Man has created God in his own image; in this way he ends up worshipping himself. This is the height of self-deception, egoism and ignorance.

The divine is not to be worshipped, the divine is to be lived. You have to have the divine in your life, not in the temple. You have to make every possible effort so that the divine can reside in your heart and pervade your every breath. For this, the disappearance of the "I" is essential. As long as your "I" remains, the divine cannot enter you. Hasn't Kabir said in one of his songs that the lane of love is very narrow and two can't move alongside each other?

One night I read until very late by the light of a lamp. When I turned off the lamp I was amazed. The full moon was shining outside, but the light of my tiny lamp had prevented the moonlight from entering my room. No sooner was my lamp extinguished than the nectar of the moonlight permeated my room. That day I came to realize that as long as the lamp of "I" is there, the light of God awaits outside the door.

The extinction of "I," the nirvana of "I" is at the same time the coming of God's light, the coming of God. Please don't construct an idol of God, just destroy the idol of "I." Its very disappearance is the appearance of God.

CHAPTER 11

A Zone of Silence

How easy it is to see truth! But the simplest things are always the most difficult to be seen. That is so because whatever is easy and near is quickly forgotten for that very reason. We remain occupied by things that are far away and lose sight of the things that are near. We remain occupied with the other and forget our own selves.

Doesn't it often happen in the theater that the audience becomes so involved in the play going on in front of them that they forget themselves? This is what has happened in life too. Life is a giant stage and we have become so engrossed in what is being acted out on the stage that we have forgotten the audience – the seer, the self. In order to attain truth, to attain your self, you only have to do one thing: you only have to wake up from the scenes, from the drama, and nothing else.

I see that you are always encircled by a kind of restlessness that is expressed in your behavior whether you are sitting, standing, walking or sleeping. It is there in your every action, small or big. Don't you feel it yourself? Have you never noticed that whatsoever you do, you are doing it restlessly?

You have to break this circle of restlessness and create a zone of silence. Only against this background of silence will you be able to experience the bliss and the music that are ever-present within you – but which has not been possible for you to hear and live because of your own inner tumult. My friends, the outer tumult is no disturbance at all. If you are at peace within, it is as if the outer tumult doesn't exist. We are restless within ourselves, that alone is the hindrance.

Someone asked me this morning, "What should we do to have peace within?" I said, "Look at the flowers. Look at how they open. Look at the mountain streams. Look at how they flow." Do you see any restlessness there? How peacefully it all goes on! There is no restlessness anywhere except in man.

You too can live like this. Live like this and experience yourself as part of nature. The belief that the "I" is separate has created all this restlessness and tension. Rid yourself completely of the "I" before you act, before you do anything. Then you will find a divine peace spreading throughout you.

When the wind is blowing be as if you are the wind, and when it rains feel that you are the rain, and then see how profound this peace gradually becomes. With the sky be the sky, with darkness be the darkness and with light be the light. Don't keep yourself separate; let the drop that you are fall into the ocean. And then you will know that which is beauty, that which is music, that which is truth.

When I walk I must be conscious that I am walking; when I stand up I must be conscious that I am standing up. No act of the body or of the mind should occur in unconsciousness, in a half-sleep. If in this way you awaken and live your life with awareness, your mind will become pure, clean, transparent.

Through such aware living and behavior, meditation pervades each activity of one's life. An inner stream of it accompanies us night and day. It calms us. It purifies our actions and makes them virtuous. Remember that a man who is awake and aware in his every action, physical or mental, cannot misbehave with others. Unconsciousness is a must for evil acts to follow. Hence, with consciousness they drop away spontaneously.

I call *samadhi*, enlightenment "the great death," and in fact that is what it is. Through ordinary death you will die – but you will be reborn because with that death your "I" will not cease to be. That "I" will take a new birth and pass through yet another death. Ordinary death is not a real death because it is followed by rebirth and death again. And this circular movement continues on and on until *samadhi*, the great death comes, and frees us from the cycle of births and deaths.

Samadhi is the great death, for it is in *samadhi* that the "I" ceases to be, and along with it the cycle of births and deaths also ceases to be. What remains then is life. Through the great death of *samadhi* one attains life immortal, where there is neither birth nor death. Immortality has neither beginning nor end. It is this great death we call *moksha*, nirvana, *brahman*.

My suggestion is to take meditation as rest and not as work nor as an activity. "Non-action" means this very thing. It is complete rest, a total halt to all actions. And when all actions cease and all the pulsations of the mind have become still, then in that restful state something begins to emerge that cannot be taught by all the religions of the world put together. The doer, which is not an action but the center and life of all actions, is seen only when there are no actions.

Sarahapada has said, "O consciousness, go and rest in the mind where even the air has no access, where the sun and the moon do not reach." Such a place is within you and nobody but you can enter. That is your atman, your soul. Your body exists up to the point where others have access. The boundary of where the world enters you is the boundary of your body. The world can enter it because your body is a part of the world; the senses are the doors through which the world enters. The mind is an accumulation of impressions, conditionings, that have entered you in this way.

That which is beyond the body, beyond the mind and the senses is the soul. Without attaining that soul life is useless, because without knowing it, without winning it, no win is a win and no attainment is an attainment.

I do not see *sansara*, "the world," and nirvana, "godliness," as two different things. The distinction that exists between them is not that of their entities. The distinction is not between them, it is in your way of looking. There are not two different entities: *sansara* and nirvana. *Sansara* and nirvana are your two ways of looking at that which is. The entity is only one but the ways of looking at it are two. Seen from the eye of knowing, it appears to be one thing; seen from the eye of ignorance, another. What appears as *sansara* in ignorance, becomes nirvana in knowing. What the world is in ignorance, is godliness in knowing. So the question is not of something on the outside, it is of the transformation within. If you change, everything else changes. You yourself are the *sansara* and the nirvana.

The truth cannot be had at any price. It cannot be obtained from others. It is the fruit of self-evolution.

Emperor Bimbisara once went to Mahavira and said, "I want to attain truth. I am willing to give anything I possess but I must have the truth that rids man of all sorrow."

Mahavira saw that the ruler wanted to conquer truth in the same way he had conquered the world, that he had the idea to buy the truth. So understanding that it was ego that has taken even this form, Mahavira said to Bimbisara, "Excellency, first go to Punya Shravak, a citizen of your empire, and get from him the fruit of one sitting of his meditation. That will clear the way for your attainment of truth and ultimate liberation."

Bimbisara went to Punya Shravak and said, "Great meditator, I have come to ask for something. I want to buy the fruit of one sitting of your meditation. I will pay whatever price you demand."

On hearing the emperor's request, Punya Shravak replied, "O

Great king, meditation means equilibrium. It means keeping the mind free from attraction and repulsion and remaining steady in one's self. How can this be given by one person to another? You want to buy it but this is impossible. You will have to acquire it yourself, there is no other way."

The truth cannot be purchased. It can neither be obtained as a gift nor received through charity. And it cannot be conquered by attack. Attacking is not the way to attain it. Attack is an attitude of ego, and where there is ego there cannot be truth. To attain truth you have to become a nothingness. Truth comes through the door of nothingness, emptiness. It doesn't come through the attack of the ego but through sensitivity and the receptivity of nothingness. One has not to attack truth, one has to prepare an opening in one-self for it to come in.

Hui-neng has said, "The way to attain truth is cultivation through non-cultivation." Non-cultivation is laid down as a condition in order to avoid the use of any force even in cultivation. It is inaction; it is non-cultivation instead of cultivation; it is not an attainment, it is a losing. The extent to which you empty yourself is the extent to which you attain.

Where does rainwater go? It doesn't remain on the hills that are full but it runs to the empty ditches. The nature of truth is similar to the nature of water. If you want to attain truth, empty yourself completely. As soon as you are empty the truth fills that empty space.

CHAPTER 12

The Discipline of Witnessing

Conscious soul,

I am very happy to see you all. I can feel the depth of your longing, of your thirst for the truth. I am seeing it in your eyes and feeling it in your every breath. And as your hearts become inspired to seek the truth, my heart is inspired too – your thirst for truth is also touching me. How delightful it is. How beautiful and juicy all this is! There is nothing sweeter, more beautiful and more beloved on earth than the longing for the truth.

In this unique moment of bliss what shall I say to you? What shall I say to you in this moment of your thirst and waiting? It is only in moments like this that we realize how insignificant, how material and non-transparent words really are. It is only in moments like this that we come to know how meaningless, incapable and powerless words are. When there is nothing really worth saying, words are able to convey it; when there is something worth saying, something profound, they are miserably inadequate. This is only natural because the realization of truth, the experience of bliss and the vision of beauty are so subtle and ethereal that no earthly form can be attributed to them. As soon as one attempts to ascribe an earthly form to them the experiences become dead and meaningless, and then the living experience does not come into our hands alive, it is its corpse that comes. The soul is left behind and whatever the words refer to is no longer the truth.

Then what shall I say? Would it have been better not to have said anything, and for you not to have heard anything at all? How nice it would have been if we had remained silent and quiet, without words, and if you could have woken up to that silence, to that emptiness and become watchful and seen something that truly is. In that case I would have been saved from speaking and you would have been saved from listening, and yet what I had intended to say would have been said without saying it. The truth would have been conveyed, because it is within everyone. The music you are searching for resounds every moment in the depths of your own being. The moments of your thirst for truth, even if they are silent, transform into a state of prayerfulness. Thirsting for God and a silent awaiting is prayer.

What man is seeking is within him. What you have gathered here to ask me about and to know from me is always within you. Neither have you ever lost it, nor can you ever lose it, because it is your very existence, your very being. That alone is the treasure that can never be lost because you yourself are it. But we are all looking for, searching for the very thing that can never be lost. How interesting. What a joke!

I am reminded of a wonderful sermon. I do not recall when or by whom it was given:

One evening there was a big gathering in a temple and a large number of monks had assembled. After a long wait the speaker arrived. As he stood up to speak, someone in the audience asked a question, "What is truth?" An alert and expectant silence filled the room. The speaker knew, hence each and every word from him mattered.

But do you know what he said? He said – and very loudly – "O monks!" An unprecedented silence resounded with these two words and every eye was on him. All were silent, watchful. But the speaker spoke no more. His speech was over; he had conveyed what he wanted to convey.

Do you understand what he said? Nothing whatsoever, wasn't it? But as I see it, he had said everything. Whatsoever is worth saying had all been covered by his speech. I too want to say the same thing. I will say only that. It alone is worth saying. That alone which words fail to say is worth saying.

Then what did he say? He said, "Don't look for truth elsewhere and don't ask anyone about it. If it exists at all, it exists within you. Otherwise it does not exist at all." So although he was asked about truth he said absolutely nothing about it. He simply called out to the assembly. He called out to them as one calls out to awaken someone from sleep. This is the only answer to the inquiry about truth. To awaken from sleep is to attain truth. There is no other way.

You are asleep, so you cannot see that which you already have, which you yourself are. And in your dreams you wander far and wide in search of it, in search of something that is already there within you, within the searcher. You are like musk-deer running around, wandering in search of musk.

But no matter how hard you search on the outside for that which lives inside you, you will not be able to find it because it cannot be attained by searching. Outer things can be attained by searching, but one cannot attain one's self with this kind of search. The truth is not found by searching, it is found by waking up. And that is why the speaker called out to the assembly and spoke no further. And for this same reason Mahavira, Buddha, Krishna and Christ have all been only calling out to you. It is not speaking, but calling. It is not a teaching, but an address, a call.

I do not intend to speak either, I intend to call. Will you hear me? Will you allow me to disturb your sleep and shatter your dreams? It may well be that your dreams are sweet, but it is the sweet dreams that are harmful, because they do not let you wake up but make the intoxication of sleep all the more intense.

I want you to become a participant in the bliss I am experiencing as the result of my awakening. And so I have decided to call you. I will not merely speak to you, I will call out to you. Pardon me if my call disturbs your sleep and disperses the fog of your dreams. I am helpless. Without shattering your dreams nothing can be said about the truth. We are engulfed in a sleep, and as long as this sleep continues all our actions are useless. As long as this sleep continues, whatever you do or you know is nothing but a dream.

The first thing is to awaken from this sleep. Everything else comes after that. Nothing precedes it. Don't attach any value to the thoughts you have learned or to the behavior you have been disciplined in during this sleep. Just look at them as happenings in a dream. While you yourself are unknown to yourself it is impossible that something right can happen from you. Your knowledge, your conduct, everything is bound to be false. Your faith, your trust, your convictions will all be blind. Whatsoever path you may walk, it will not lead to the truth. In fact, there is no question of your walking at present. Does anybody walk a path while asleep? It is only a dream about walking.

The ignorance of the self is the sleep I am talking to you about. It is necessary to awaken from it. In order to wake up from this sleep it is also necessary to understand the factors that do not allow you to wake up. Before knowing religion it is necessary to know what religion is not and also to understand what you are holding onto as religion. This religion is more like a sleeping pill than a means for awakening.

Karl Marx has called religion "the opium of the people." Religion is certainly not a drug, but what is generally mistaken for religion is nothing but that. Marx was mistaken in branding religion as opium and you are mistaken in branding opium as religion. It is essential to understand what religion is and what opium is.

Let us first consider what religion is not and then you will experience what religion is. Just contemplation is enough to make irreligion evaporate. But about religion, contemplation alone is not enough; religion comes through spiritual endeavor.

Let me tell you one thing. If you really wish to make some progress in your religious life, you must begin by not carrying any belief. If you wish to know the truth, you should not create any preconceived notions about it. You must approach truth in complete peace and emptiness, and without any preconceptions. Preconceived notions and biases dim and distort your vision. What you know then is not the truth but a projection of your own thinking. That way truth does not reveal itself to you, on the contrary you impose yourself on truth.

When there is no particular view or theory between you and the truth, what you will know then will be the truth. Otherwise you are not able to get out of the boundary of your mind and you go on knowing things as you want to know them. This is not knowledge, this is imagination.

Man has an unlimited power for imagination and this imagination alone is the wall between him and the truth. If you have preconceived ideas about God, truth and the soul, your mind will form an image of them and you will think that you have known something. But the reality is that you have known nothing and have wandered only in the realms of imagination. This is not seeing the truth, but a dream.

You know very well that your mind has an inexhaustible capacity for dreaming. Our desires show us things that do not exist at all. They create mirages: that which truly is becomes hidden and that which is not becomes apparent.

But you will say that dreaming happens only in sleep. It is

true that dreams happen only in sleep, but sleep can be induced, and in one sense you can be asleep while you are awake. Don't you daydream?

So, if you continuously create a particular idea of God or truth and, awake or asleep, are filled with the remembrance of these imaginings, then certainly a projection happens and it even becomes visible. It is nothing but an intensified daydream. There is nothing actually in front of your eyes, but what has been nourished and nurtured behind the eyes for a long time becomes visible. This is a projection; this is how dreams are seen, this is how the realization of truth based on preconceptions becomes possible.

A devotee of Christ sees Christ, a follower of Krishna sees Krishna and someone else's disciples sees someone else. By no means is this the vision or realization of God or of truth. This is a projection of one's own imagination because there cannot be two truths, two Gods. Truth is one and its realization is one, and one who wants to know truth must give up his countless concepts and imaginings.

I am not asking you to give up your concepts in favor of some other concept, I am asking you to give up all concepts as such. These very concepts are the lifeline of all the sects that exist in the name of religion, and because of this, there are many sects but there is no religion.

To know the truth it is necessary to forsake all theories about it, because only in such an unbiased, unprejudiced and therefore innocent state, can that which is be known. Where there is no pre-concept, no prior imagination, no prior expectation, that is where no dreams form and the truth is realized. So, the discipline of truth-realization is not in fact the discipline of truth-realization, rather it is the discipline of dream-riddance.

It is not the realization of truth, it is simply freedom from hallucinations. That freedom is the realization of truth. We are lost in dreams, hence that which is, is almost an absence despite its constant presence.

Truth simply is, because what else is truth but that which is? It does not need to be brought from somewhere else. It is ever-present. But we are not present to it because we are lost in our dreams. No, it is not the truth we have to bring to ourselves, we have to bring ourselves to the truth. This is possible not by seeing more new dreams about God, but by doing away with all the dreams – by waking up.

Hence I said that the truth does not need imagination, but a realization that when the mind is free from all imagination it is then in the state of truth. The world is the realization of a choosing mind; truth is the realization of a non-choosing mind.

All concepts and all beliefs are choices and therefore not gateways to the truth. They are obstacles and lead nowhere. On the contrary, they block your path. The path to truth does not lie through them but beyond them.

So don't form any idea, concept, sketch or conviction about truth. The belief you form will become an experience. But that experience is not real, only mental. These experiences are not spiritual. All beliefs taught in your ignorance to discover truth are false. Don't think about what truth is and what it is like. All such thinking is blind. It is like a blind man trying to imagine light. Poor thing – how can he conceive what light is! Without eyesight, thinking about light is not possible. Whatever such a person may think will be fundamentally wrong. He cannot even imagine darkness accurately, let alone light. One needs eyes to see darkness as well.

What shall a man without eyesight do then? I would say to him, "Don't think about light. Treat your eyes." It isn't thinking but treatment that can be helpful and meaningful. But what do I see? I see him being given sermons, I see the philosophy about light being explained to him. But nobody bothers about treating his eyes.

And what is more surprising is that those who are sermonizing on the subject of light have not seen the light themselves!

They too know about the existence of light, but they have not known light. I say this because if they had known light they would have realized the futility of all sermons and would have focused their concern and sympathy on the treatment for blindness. If the eyesight is cured, light is experienced automatically. Light is ever-present, what is required is eyesight. If there is no sight, the presence of light turns into absence.

Sight and *light* are words that can lead in very different directions. Thinking about light leads to philosophy. It is the dimension of mere thinking. It does not lead to experience; it is mere thinking. There is a lot of walking in it but one reaches nowhere. There are many conclusions but never the ultimate conclusion that brings the solution in life. This is only natural. Even the most perfect thinking process about water cannot quench one's smallest thirst. The path to quench one's thirst is quite different. It is having a discipline for eyesight, not thinking about light. I have said that thinking about light is philosophy and now I want to say that having a discipline for eyesight is religion. By thinking you can attain intellectual conclusions, while through meditation you attain spiritual experience. One is like thinking about water; the other, like quenching one's thirst. One is still part of the problem; the other is the solution.

I ask everyone this question: Do you want to know light or to know about light? Do you want to know truth or do you want to know about truth? Do you want to know about water or do you want to quench your thirst? Your answer to these questions will decide whether you are thirsty for knowing or for collecting information.

And keep in your remembrance that these two are opposite directions. One leads to ego-dissolution; the other to ego-enhancement. One makes you innocent while the other makes you complicated. True knowledge destroys the ego whereas information pumps it up and inflates it all the more. All collecting, all acquiring fills the ego, and for this reason the ego desires it, lusts after it.

Thoughts are also a subtle form of acquisition, a food for the ego. The conceit you find among scholars is not without reason, nor is it accidental. It is the natural outcome of thought accumulation.

Thoughts are accumulated. They come from the outside, they do not arise within you. Hence, they are not of the soul, of the being, but are only an outer covering. Information about light can be given to a blind man from the outside, but the sensation of light has to arise in him from within. One is an acquirement, and the other an energy, a sense faculty. The difference between information and knowing is that of acquirement and innate energy. Acquirement comes from the outside; energy, power comes from within.

Acquirement gives the illusion of power. This illusion is quite strong and it nourishes the ego. Egoism is not power, it is an illusion of power. In fact, it is a non-power, because merely one ray of truth destroys it, evaporates it. This is why true power is always found to be free of egoism.

I hope you have been able to understand the distinction between learning and wisdom. It is imperative you understand it. False knowledge is an even greater hindrance on the path of self-realization than ignorance. Knowledgeability is false knowledge. False knowledge is to have the impression that "I know" when you really don't. Such an illusion easily grows out of the acquisition of others' thoughts. This false impression comes out of a knowledge of the scriptures, out of a knowledge of words. And because of this knowledge of words, man slowly, slowly starts feeling that he has known the truth. Words become a part of his memory and he seems to know the answers to all questions.

One's intelligence gets suppressed under borrowed ideas, and before one can look for an answer in one's interiority, a ready-made answer pops out from the layer of borrowed words and ideas. In this way one is saved the trouble of living out the problem but is consequently deprived of the solution as well.

If a problem is mine it is my solution alone that is required. No borrowed or secondhand solution can be of any help.

One can neither borrow life nor the solutions to its problems. The solution to a problem does not come from outside of it. It grows out of the problem itself. If the problem is within, the truth cannot be outside. Hence the truth cannot be learned, it has to be uncovered, it has to be discovered. It isn't through education but by spiritual endeavor that the truth can be known. This is the fundamental difference between the scholar and the self-realized one. It is enough to be well versed in "scriptures" pertaining to the world, but it is not so in the realm of the soul – in that realm it is not even the beginning.

You can only have information about the world, matter and the other. You cannot have knowing about these things that are outside of you. Anything that is outside of you can be known only superficially, from its outside. No matter how close you are to it, you will still be at a distance. However small this distance may be, it will never close completely. So you can only become *familiar* with things that are not your self, but you cannot *know* them. You can know *about* them, but you cannot know the things themselves.

The total absence of distance is the prerequisite for knowing, because it is only then that you can enter into the inner being of that entity. But anything that has a distance can never become non-distant. The distance can only cease with an entity that has no distance from the knower. Distance can be eliminated only if it is illusory. If it is real, its elimination is not possible.

There is one and only one entity that has no distance from you. It is impossible for this entity to have a distance from you. You *yourself* are that entity. Only this entity can be known. Any distance from this entity is an illusion, because how can there be any distance from your own self? You alone are the center of yourself to which you have absolute access – and that is your inner abode. Only this point can be known, only this can become your knowing.

May I also remind you that we cannot know the world, we can only have an acquaintance with it, information about it. And there can be no information about the self, we can only know it. That is why, in the case of matter, in the case of the material world, it is enough to be an expert in the scriptures, but it is not so in the case of the self. Science is scripture; religion is not. Science is information about matter, while religion is a knowing of the self. Science is a scripture; religion is a spiritual discipline.

I do not preach. That dimension is totally fruitless. What is required is not preaching but a treatment. It is not that doctrines about truth should be given. They are altogether useless. What is of value is the method, the technique by which one can see truth. A technique serves as a treatment and because of it the eyes open. Then you don't have to think about light, you see it. When eyes are absent you have to think, but when there are eyes, thinking is out of the question. In blindness, thinking tries to do the work of the eyes, but as soon as the eyes are restored thinking becomes unnecessary.

In my viewpoint, thinking is not a symptom of true knowledge but of ignorance. True knowledge is a state of thoughtlessness. It is not thinking, it is insight. And no doctrine about truth can give you this insight. At its best that remains merely an intellectual acquisition. It can become part of the memory, but it can never become knowledge.

Doctrines can be taught but they never bring a transformation to one's personality. Like clothing, they effect a change on the surface but the interior remains what it was. The inner being remains untouched by them, only the outer cover takes on a new form and a new color. In this way man does not awaken into wisdom. On the contrary, he falls into the ditch of hypocrisy. A great gulf between his state of being and his knowledge is created. He is one thing and what he knows is quite another thing. His personality is split in two. There is a conflict, and a duality is created between his inner being and his outer layer. And the natural result of this is hypocrisy. Such a man begins to pretend to be that which is not really there within him, and begins to hide that which he is. This acting is not religiousness. It destroys no one's life but his own. This is self-deception, but this is what is taken and taught as religiousness.

Mere intellectual teachings of dogmas, of doctrines, can only do this much: they can only change the outer covering. For a self-revolution some other dimension is needed. That dimension is not of doctrines but of endeavors toward self-realization. It is not the dimension of sermonizing but of treatment. It is not the dimension of thinking about truth but of opening your eyes to truth.

Religion is the method for opening your eyes. Once your eyes open, then seeing that which is becomes easy. But doctrines will not open your eyes. On the contrary, those who are deluded by them forget that their eyes are still closed and that the truths they are talking about have not been seen by them with their own eyes but by the eyes of somebody else. The truth seen by somebody else is like a meal eaten by somebody else. It serves no purpose whatsoever for others.

The realization of truth is absolutely private and individual and is by no means transferable. It can neither be received nor given. It has to be attained by oneself. It cannot be stolen or accepted in charity. It is not a piece of property, it is one's own self. Truth is not property, it is one's own self and it is therefore non-transferable. To this day no one has ever given it to anyone. Nor will anybody ever be able to give it to anyone in the future because the moment it is given it will cease to be the truth, it will become a thing, an object. Only a thing can be given or taken. Truth has to be attained within oneself, by oneself. In fact, it is not even an "attainment," it is only "being" it. It is your own *isness*, your own existence.

So where does the question of learning truth come in? It only has to be uncovered. Learning only forms more layers over the self. All outside teachings only cover truth. Whatsoever comes from the outside can only cover. Covering is the only possibility from the outside. And the garments of thought keep covering the self more and more. You have to strip off these garments and be naked. In order to know your self, you have to throw all garments away. In order to know your self you have to unlearn, not learn. When all the outside guests have gone you will know the one who is not a guest, but the host.

The truth cannot be taught but the *method* of knowing truth can be. Today, no one speaks of this method. Although there is a lot of talk about truth, there is no talk about the method of seeing the truth. There can be no greater mistake than this. It is like leaving life aside and clinging to the body. As a result of this there are many, many religions, but no religion as such.

The numerous sects that masquerade under the name of religions are not religion at all. There can only be one religion. There can be no adjective attached to it. There can be no qualifying term to it. Religion means religion, there cannot be "such and such" a religion and "this and this" religion. Where there is "such and such" and "this and this" there is no religion.

These sects have come into being because of the doctrines and theories about truth. They will continue to exist as long as there is emphasis and insistence on theories and doctrines. Doctrine is an insistence on words. Sects form around these very words. The words become causes of conflict, feeding animosities and petty hates. These words divide man from man. And how strange it is that people believe that the very words that divide man from man will unite man with the divine! That which divides man from man cannot possibly unite him with himself, with truth, nor with the divine.

This fall of religion into sects is because of doctrines, because of words, because of beliefs and concepts. This fall is based on ignorance and not on knowledge. Truth has no sect. All sects belong to doctrines. Realization of truth becomes freedom from sects. And at that very moment one enters religion – the religion that is not Hindu or Jaina, or Christian or Moham-medan, but simply religion, simply light, simply consciousness. Religion is the realization of one's self.

A sect is not religious. What does religion have to do with organization? All organizations are political or social; organizations as such are worldly. They are based on fear of each other and where there is fear there is hatred. They come into existence not out of truth, but out of the need for security. Whether it is a nation, a society or a sect, all are born out of fear. And the function of what is born out of fear is to cause fear in others.

All sects are doing exactly this. They do not intend to make anyone religious, they want to increase their numbers. Numbers are power and assurances of security. Numbers are for both self-protection and for providing the capacity to attack. Sects have been doing nothing else but this all along; they are still doing this and they will continue to do this. They haven't united man with religion, they have torn him away from it.

Religion is not a social phenomenon, it is absolutely a personal revolutionary transformation. It has nothing to do with others; it is concerned with oneself alone. It isn't concerned with what a man does with others but what he does with himself. Religion is concerned with what one does with oneself in one's absolute alone-ness.

What you are in your absolute aloneness is what you must know. Who you are is what you must know. Only the realization of your own being will lead you to religion. There is no other way to lead someone to religion. No temple, no mosque, no church can take you to the place where you already are. You don't have to climb any outside stairs to get there. All temples are outside, all temples are part of the world, and you cannot reach the self through their doors. No journey in the outer world can be a pilgrimage to the holy place. That place is within, where you have the experience of religion and where mystery, bliss, beauty and life are revealed. Without this everything is a misery; everything is useless, meaningless.

In order to know the self one has to go inside, not outside. But all man's senses take him outward. They are all outgoing. His eyes look outward, his hands spread outward, his legs move outward and even his mind reflects and echoes the external. This is why he has created idols and images of God, and has erected temples to truth – it is so that his eyes can see God and his feet can make a pilgrimage to truth. We have created this self-deception ourselves; we have taken this cup of poison with our own hands. And we waste away our lives and spend them in stupor brought about by this poison and self-deception.

To suit the convenience of our senses we have imagined and created religion outside ourselves, whereas the reality is that in order to know religion we have to go behind the senses. If you want to know the knower, the consciousness that knows the world through the medium of the senses, you cannot do it through the same medium. The knower itself cannot be known in the same manner as the objects of knowing are. The seer, the consciousness, cannot itself be seen as an object of seeing. Subjectivity can never be reduced to, degraded to objectivity. The whole problem is that this simple fact has not been understood. People search for God as if he were an external object. Journeys to mountains and forests take place as if God were an external object. How insane this is! God is not to be searched for, he is hidden in the seeker himself, he is attained the moment the seeker is known.

Truth is within you. It is within me. It is not that it will be within you tomorrow, it is in you here and now, at this very moment. I am; this *isness* itself is my truth. Whatever else I see may not be a truth, it may all be only a dream – because I do see dreams and while I see them they appear to be true. So this whole world that is seen may be only a dream. You may all be a dream for me. It may well be that I am in a dream and you are not really here. But the seer cannot be unreal. The seer itself cannot be a dream, because if it were then it would not be possible for it to dream. A dream cannot see a dream. An unreality cannot know unreality. In order to see a dream someone who is not a dream is required. Even to see unreality a real seer is a must. Therefore I say I am the truth. Truth is my being. I don't have to go anywhere to search for it.

You only have to dig out the truth from within yourself. Just as you dig out a well, you have to dig out the truth. There are always a few layers of stones and earth covering a spring of water, but as soon as you remove those layers the spring is attained. In the same way your self is pressed down by layers of "other." You only have to break through those layers and what you have been searching for through countless past lives is attained. You have been unable to attain it so far because you have been searching for it far away, while in fact it is very close to you – it is the one who is searching.

You must dig out the well of your soul. And meditation is the instrument with which to do that. With the tool of meditation you have to remove the layers of the earth of "otherness" that have piled up on the self. This alone is the remedy, the only treatment. This is what I want to talk about.

First of all, it is necessary to know what it is that has covered up your own self, your intrinsic self-nature. What is it that hides you from yourself? Don't you see it? Don't you understand this covering layer? When you go inside who or what do you find?

Hume has said, "Whenever I have gone inside I have found nothing but thoughts." Hume did not find any soul, nor will you find yours in this way. Hume saw only the covering layers and came back; he went only as far as the shell and returned. It is only when you break the shell open that you will see what is inside. This is just like a man who goes to a lake and seeing the surface covered with moss and leaves returns to say that there is no lake at all. Generally this is what happens. You go inside every day, you see the covering of thoughts that are constantly there and you return. You know nothing except thoughts. Thoughts are your whole world. And he who lives in thoughts alone is a worldly man. To know something beyond thoughts is the beginning of becoming religious. To know the state of thoughtlessness, is to enter the domain of religion.

It may be that your thoughts are not about this world but are about the soul, about God, and you may be under the illusion that you are religious. I want to destroy this illusion of yours. Thoughts as such are a covering, an outer shell. They are all desires, because they are external, outer. There can be no thought about the self. There is knowing about the self, but not thought. Thoughts are the covering. Thoughtlessness can uncover the self.

To be without thoughts is meditation. When there are no thoughts, we come to know the one hidden by our thoughts. When there are no clouds the blue sky is revealed. My friends, there is a sky within you as well. Remove the cloud of thoughts so that it can be seen, so that it can be known. This is possible. When the mind is at rest and there are no thoughts in it, then in that silence, in that deep thoughtlessness, in that choiceless state truth is seen.

What can we do to bring this about? A very simple thing has to be done but you will find it very difficult because you have become very complex. Something that is possible even for a newborn baby has become impossible for you. You have to look at the world and at yourself in the same way as a newborn baby looks. The baby simply looks and does not think. He just sees. And just seeing is wonderful. This is the secret key that can unlock the gate of truth.

I am seeing you. I am just seeing you. Do you follow me? I am just seeing you; I am not thinking. And then an unprecedented calm, a living silence descends within. Then everything is seen and everything is heard but nothing within moves. There is no reaction inside; there are no thoughts. There is only *darshan*, only seeing.

Right-seeing, right-awareness is the method for meditation. You have to see, only to see all that is without and all that is within as well. There are objects without, thoughts within. You have to look at them without any purpose whatsoever. There is no purpose, there is only seeing. You are a witness, an uninvolved witness, and you are simply seeing. This observing, this watchfulness, gradually leads you into peace, into utter emptiness, into thoughtlessness. Try it and find out. As thoughts dissolve, consciousness awakens and comes to life. Just casually stop for a while – anywhere, anytime. Just look and listen and be a witness to the world and to yourself. Don't think, just be a witness and then see what happens. Then let this witnessing spread. Let it pervade all your physical and mental activities. Allow it to be with you continuously. If there is witnessing, you will cease to be and you will see that which you really are. The "I" will die and the self will be attained.

In this discipline of witnessing, in this observing of one's neutral watcher, an effortless transition, an easy changeover happens from what is being witnessed to the one who is witnessing. As you observe your thoughts you begin to get glimpses of the one that is observing. And then one day when the seer appears in his full majesty and glory, all your poverty and wretchedness come to an end.

This is not a discipline that one can practice only once in a while and then become liberated. This has to be practiced continuously, night and day. Gradually it will pervade you all the time. As you practice witnessing, as you move more into the state of witnessing, that state settles more and more and begins to be present all the time. Sitting or standing, walking or stopping, it is present. Slowly it remains there both in waking and sleeping states. It continues to be present even in sleep. And when this happens, when it begins to be present even in sleep, you can be certain that it has deepened, that it has gone deep within.

As of now you are asleep even when you are awake, then

you will be awake even when you are sleeping.

The discipline of witnessing disperses thoughts from the waking state and dreams from sleep. The mind free of thoughts and dreams is unstirred. It becomes calm, waveless, without a tremor, just as the sea is calm when there are no waves, just as the flame of a lamp does not flicker when there is no breeze blowing into the house. It is in such a state that the self – that which one is, that which is the truth – is known. And the gates to the palace of God open.

This gate, this entrance, does not lie in the scriptures, in words – it lies within oneself. That is why I say not to search elsewhere but to dig within yourself. Don't go anywhere else. Go inside yourself. I have explained to you the method of how to go in.

From the serenity and the sparkle that has descended in your eyes I conclude you have understood me. But this understanding alone is not enough. It is not intellectual understanding, but spiritual experience which becomes the foundation for a life of truth. Walk a bit in the direction of what I have said and see. Just be a little in that dimension and see. Even if you only walk a little you will have gone a long way because when you move toward the truth, with every move you make toward it, you keep coming more under the influence of its gravitational pull – and you not only walk toward it, but get drawn by it as well.

And finally, remember that those who walk certainly reach one day. No step taken in God's direction ever goes in vain. I bear witness to this truth. How I want you also to realize this truth, even for a moment, so that you can bear witness to it as well! It is so close to you. It is just a matter of your waking up to it. The sun has already risen. You only have to open your eyes to see it.

I am inviting you to open your eyes. Will you hear my call and open your eyes? The decision and determination depend on you and you alone.

CHAPTER 13

The Dewdrop and the Ocean

Osho,
Don't you attach any value to philosophy? In order to
know the truth is it not necessary to know about the
truth?

The truth cannot be known before you actually know it. And
to know about truth is not knowing truth. All that knowing is
false. It is false because in the absence of one's own experience it
simply cannot be understood. It is false, not necessarily from the
side of the speaker, but from that of the listener.

If I say anything about truth, will you understand it in
exactly the same way as I am saying it? It isn't possible, because
to understand something in exactly the same way you would
have to be the same as me and in the same place as I am. By the
time what I say reaches to you it becomes untrue. This is how it
always happens. I only give you the words, their interpretation
will come from within you. The meaning will be born from
within you and it cannot be anything other than from you. The
words will be mine; their meaning will be yours.

That meaning cannot be anything more than you, it cannot be beyond your experience. Do you think you are reading Krishna when you read the Gita? If you do, you are greatly mistaken, my friend! You are only reading yourself in the Gita – otherwise how could there have been so many interpretations of it, so many commentaries on it? In every scripture, you manage to see your own image and every religion is nothing more than a mirror to you.

Before knowing truth only words can be known, not the truth. Those words will be from others, from the holy books, from the *avataras* and *tirthankaras*, from the enlightened ones, but the meanings and interpretations will be yours. It is you who will be in them. Isn't this the reason that there is so much antagonism, that there are so many differences between the so-called religions? Is there any opposition or antagonism possible between Buddha and Christ? The difference of interpretation, the opposition, the antagonism is ours, and we just continue it in their names.

Religion comes from those who know the truth, and sects are formed and organized by those who only hear it, who only believe in it. And so there are numerous sects – although there is only one religion. The reason is that the experience of knowing the truth is an identical experience for all, but the belief in truth cannot be identical. Knowing is one, but beliefs are as many as there are persons who believe.

Religion is born out of seeing the truth, realizing the truth, but religions are born out of not seeing the truth. The wheel of religion is moved by those who know, but organizing religions is the act of those who do not know – and it is through their good efforts that religion becomes irreligion. Throughout his whole history man has been a victim of this calamity.

Osho,
But without forming some concept about truth we just cannot even think about it.

I am not asking you to think at all. Thinking never goes beyond what you already know. And if you don't know truth how can you possibly think about it? Thinking always stays within the boundaries of your experience. Thinking is just chewing over your knowledgeability. Thinking is never creative, it is merely repetitive. What is unknown cannot be known by thinking. If you want to know the unknown you must get out of what you know. To enter the unknown you have to leave the shores of the known.

It is therefore better not to form any concept of truth at all. That concept will be totally untrue – lifeless, not a living meaning. That concept may receive respect from the traditions, may become revered by thousands, may be supported by scriptures, but for you it will have no value at all. For the seeker of truth, it is not only valueless but false.

It is one thing to see the fragmented sky of truth through the confinement of the window frame of that concept, and quite another to come out from all confinements and window frames and look at the whole expanse of the sky.

The sky is not confined by anything. Nor is the truth confined by anything. All confinements are man-made; all concepts are man-made. All words given to it are by man. Truth is that which is not man-made. If you want to know the truth, step out of your confinements and frames. Step out of all words, and thoughts and knowledgeability. Let go of the known so that the unknown can enter in. And leave behind all man-created concepts so that you can experience that which is uncreated – the basis of all creation itself.

Osho,
How can we possibly know truth without the help of
the scriptures? Isn't it only through them that we can
know truth?

Do you mean to say that if all the scriptures were destroyed the truth would be destroyed? Is truth dependent on the scriptures or are the scriptures dependent on truth? My friend, the truth has never been attained by means of the scriptures. On the contrary, the scriptures were obtained, were revealed after the truth had been realized. It is not the scriptures that are of value, it is the truth which is of value. The fundamental thing is the truth, not the scriptures. And if truth could be attained through the scriptures it would be a very cheap thing indeed. You could attain it without making any change in yourself.

But the scriptures can only fill your memory, they cannot give you any realization on their own. And in the dimension of truth nothing happens through memory training. For truth, you have to pay the price of self-transformation. The scriptures can only make you a pundit, a scholar, they cannot give birth to knowing in you. From scriptures more scriptures can be born. This is only natural. The material can only produce the material. But how can knowing be born out of the scriptures? Knowing is the nature of consciousness, it cannot arise out of unconscious matter. The scriptures are without life, without consciousness, truth is not so. The scriptures can only enrich the unconscious, lifeless memory. Conscious knowing cannot be attained by going into them, but by going into oneself.

I will say how can you know the truth as long as there are scriptures in between? This false notion that truth can be obtained from someone else, from the scriptures or from a guru, does not allow you to search for it within yourself. This idea is a big obstacle. This search is still in the world. Remember that the scriptures are part of the world as well. Whatever is outside is the world. The truth is where there is no outside – it is within, where the self is. The self is the real scripture. It is also the only real guru. By entering the self, truth is attained.

Osho,
Is what intellect suggests to be the truth not the truth?

Intellect thinks. Intellect is not knowing. Thinking is groping in the dark, it is not knowing. The truth cannot be thought – it is seen, realized. This does not happen through the intellect but when the intellect is quiet and empty. This state of inner knowing is not intellect, it is intuition. Intuition is not thinking, it is an eye. To one who wants to see truth, intuition is like acquisition of sight to a blind man. No one ever gets anywhere by thinking. It is an endless groping. A blind man may grope endlessly but will he be able to attain to the light because of his groping? Just as there is no relation between groping and light, there is none between thinking and truth. They are altogether different dimensions.

Osho,
Do you not consider a vision of Krishna or of Christ a spiritual experience?

No, this is not a spiritual experience. No vision is a spiritual experience. On that level all experiences are psychological. As long as there is the vision of someone else there is no vision of the self. Even in such experiences you are still outside your self, you have still not come into your self. That coming into one's self takes place when there are no outer experiences whatsoever. When there is no object in front of the consciousness it settles effortlessly into itself. Only a consciousness without object can settle on the self.

Outside myself I am surrounded by two worlds: the world of matter and the world of the mind. Both of these are outside me. Not only is matter outside, the mind is outside as well. Because the mind is inside the body, it creates the illusion of being inner, but it is not. The self is inner, behind the mind, beyond the mind.

We do not mistake material experiences for spiritual experiences, but our psychological experiences do create the illusion of being spiritual because the mental images we see are different from those of the material world we know and because we also see them after we have closed our eyes. But among psychological experiences, we do not consider dreams to be spiritual experiences, even though they too only appear when we shut our eyes and even though any waking, any contact with the outside world, puts an end to them.

Only those psychological experiences that create the illusion of being real and spiritual are called "mental projections." The mind has the capacity to hypnotize itself to such a degree that it can see the dreams it sees with closed eyes even after the eyes have been opened. This happens in a kind of waking sleep. Thus we see God as we want to – Krishna or Christ. Such visions are only mental projections in which we don't see what really is, but whatsoever it is we wish to see. These experiences are neither spiritual nor of the divine. They are simply psychological experiences and are caused by self-hypnosis.

Osho,
How is God seen then?

This word *seeing* is misleading. It gives an impression as if God is a person who will be seen. Similarly the word *God* also creates the illusion of a person, a personality. There is no God, there is only *godliness*. God is not a person, only energy. God is an infinite ocean of energy, an infinite ocean of consciousness which is manifesting itself in all forms. God is not separate as some creator, it is the creation, it is creativity, it is life.

Surrounded by the ego, we create the illusion that we are separate from this life. This is our distance, our separation from godliness. In actuality, there is no distance or separation. The illusion created by the "I" is the distance. This distance is ignorance. In fact, there is no distance as such, ignorance itself is the distance.

Once the "I" dissolves, an infinite, boundless, creative life force is realized and that is "God." The experience one has at the death of "I" is the seeing of God. What you see is that the "I" is nowhere, and that which is in the waves of the ocean is in you; that which is in the fresh spring shoots is in you; that which is in autumn's falling leaves is in you. You are nowhere discontinuous and separate from the universal *isness*, you are in it; you are it. This experience is called "seeing God."

A seer has said, *"Tattvamasi svetaketu"* – That art thou. The day you feel and experience this, you have realized God. Anything less then this, different from this, is all imagination.

What vision of God can you have? One has to become God oneself. What vision of the ocean can a dewdrop have? – but it can lose its identity and become the ocean itself. As long as it is a dewdrop there is a vast gap between it and the ocean, but once it loses its identity and dissolves in the ocean, it is itself the ocean.

Do you search *for* God? Seek how to *become* God. And the path of this search is the same as the dewdrop's in its search for the ocean.

Osho,
I believe in God, but you say belief is harmful. Should I give up my belief?

Isn't the answer to your question present in the question itself? What kind of belief is this that one can hold on to or give up at wish? It is just a blind mental concept which clearly has no value at all. That is blind faith and the less blindness you have in life the better.

I do not ask you to believe, I ask you to know. Only a state of mind that comes through knowing, through realizing, has any value. You can call it "right faith" if you wish, but it is not faith, it is knowing. Don't have faith in truth, search for it, seek it out. But don't catch hold of any belief or concept. This is a sign of the mind's weakness. It is lethargy; it is a negligence. It is an injurious way to save yourself from the work of seeking it out for yourself.

Blind faith is an escape from the endeavor for self-realization. In a sense it is nothing short of suicide, because once one falls into this ditch one becomes incapable of climbing the peak of truth. These two paths lead you in opposite directions. One is the ditch you fall into, the other, the lofty summit you climb to.

Faith is an easy thing because a man is not required to do anything. In that sense, knowing is not so easy. Knowing is the complete transformation of life. Faith is merely an outer apparel; knowing is the inner revolution. The easiness of faith naturally throws religion from the fire of spiritual endeavor into the slumber of blind belief. Religion is not about faith, but unfortunately the mob religions of today are just that. And that is why what seems to be "mob religion" is what I find myself unable to call religion. About that only Karl Marx is right: it is not religion, but opium.

CHAPTER 14

Birth of a New Man

You have been told to have faith in the scriptures, faith in the words of God, faith in the religious teachers. I don't say this at all. I say: have faith in yourself. It is only by knowing yourself that you can know what there is in the scriptures, what the words of God are. One who has no faith in himself finds all his other beliefs meaningless. Can you stand on someone else's feet if you cannot stand on your own? Buddha has said: "Be a light unto yourself. Be your own refuge. There is no right refuge except the refuge of one's own self." I say the same thing.

One night a certain monk was bidding farewell to another monk who had been his guest when the latter said, "The night is very dark. How can I see to go?" The host lit a lamp and gave it to his guest. But as the guest was going down the staircase the host blew out the lamp. The place was enveloped in darkness again. Then the host said, "My lamp will not be able to light your path. For that you must have a lamp of your own." The guest understood the monk's advice, and this understanding became the birth of a light on the path of his life that could never be extinguished nor taken away.

Spiritual discipline is not just a part, a fragment of life, it is the whole of it. Your standing, sitting, speaking, laughing has all to be encompassed by it. Only then is it meaningful and natural. Religion is not found in any particular act, like worship or prayer, it is a way of living in which your whole life becomes a worship, a prayer. It is not a ritual, it is a way of life. In this sense, no religion is religious, it is the individual who becomes religious. No behavior is religious, one's life is religious.

Only by becoming free from the bondage of the ego, of the "I," does consciousness rise above the individual and become one with the whole. Just as an earthen jar separates ocean water from the ocean, the mortal enclosure of the ego keeps the individual away from the truth.

What is this ego, this "I"? Have you ever searched for it in yourself? It is there only because you have never looked for it. When I tried to find it myself, I discovered that it did not exist.

In some quiet moment go within yourself and look. No "I" is found anywhere. The "I" does not exist. It is a mere illusion ushered into being because of its social utility. Just as you have a name, you have your ego too. Both are utilities, not truths. That which is within you has neither name nor ego.

There is no such thing as entering into nirvana, into *moksha*, into liberation, into the soul. Because how can you enter a place you have never left? So then, what happens? There is no such thing as an entry into nirvana, but what happens is that the world you were immersed in dissolves like a dream and you find yourself in your self. This experience is not at all like entering some place, it is more like finding yourself on your bed at the abrupt termination of a journey you were taking in a dream. Since you haven't gone anywhere, there is no question of returning; since you haven't lost anything, all talk of attaining is meaningless. You are only dreaming a dream; all your ideas of having gone away and having lost something are only in a dream. So you neither have to return anywhere nor to find anything. You only have to wake up.

The realization of truth is always perfect and total. It is not a gradual attainment. It is not evolution, it is revolution. Does anyone awaken from a dream gradually? Either there is a dream or there is no dream. There is no middle stage.

Yes, spiritual discipline may take a long, long time but the realization of truth happens like a flash of lightning – in a split moment and in all its completeness. Realization does not involve any part of time as such, because whatever happens in time is always gradual. Spiritual discipline is in the realm of time, but realization is not. It is beyond time.

For the realization of truth, merely practicing goodness and non-attachment is not enough. That is a partial spiritual discipline. For the realization of truth, it is essential to rise above both good and evil, attachment and non-attachment, the world and nirvana. That state is called *veetaragata*, the state beyond both attachment and non-attachment. *Veetaragata* consciousness is the state where there is neither attachment nor non-attachment, neither good nor evil, but where there is only consciousness in its purity, in itself. It is in this space that realization of truth happens.

You have to cultivate a detached and wakeful mind. You have to instill this mental state in yourself in such a way that it is interwoven like your breath, night and day. You are to be wakeful and detached in every activity – this has been called no-action in action. It is just the way an actor in a play, who is alert about the acting, does not become identified with the character and lose his sense of reality. Although acting, he remains detached. This is how you have to become and be.

If a man is wakeful while engaged in activity it is not difficult for him to remain detached. It is the natural outcome of wakefulness. You are walking on a road. If you are fully wakeful to the act of walking, you will feel as if you are walking and yet not walking. The walking is happening only on the plane of the body, there is no walking on the plane of consciousness. You will feel the same while eating or while doing other things. A center within you will remain just a witness. It will neither be the doer nor the enjoyer. The deeper the intensity of this experience of witnessing becomes, the more the feelings of happiness and of sorrow will disappear – and you will realize the non-dual, pure consciousness that is your soul.

What is the mind? It is the collection and the collector of whatever is perceived by the senses. He who considers this mind as his self has mistaken the servant for the master. He who wants to realize his self will have to let go of all that he knows and follow the knower in him. All that one knows is one's mind, and *with what* one knows is the self.

It is the witness – the knower – which is the self. This self is separate from birth and death, separate from maya and *moksha*, world and liberation. It is only a witness, a witness to everything – to light, to darkness, to the world, to nirvana. This self is beyond *all* dualities. The truth is, this self is even beyond the self and the other, because it is a witness to them as well.

As soon as someone knows this witness he becomes like a lotus – separate from the mud out of which it was born and untouched by the water in which it lives. Such a man is calm and composed in all life's varied situations – in pleasure and in pain, in honor and in humiliation – because he is only a witness. Whatever happens it does not happen to him, it happens in front of him. He becomes just like a mirror which reflects thousands of images but on which no mark of any of them is left behind.

An old monk came to the shore of a river with a young companion. The young man asked, "How shall we cross this river?" The old man replied, "In such a way that your feet don't get wet." The young man heard him and like a flash of lightning something became very clear and evident to him. The river had come and gone but the mysterious maxim had penetrated deeply into his heart. It became the guiding principle and style of his life. Because of this he learned to cross the river in a way that his feet did not get wet.

Become a person who eats and yet is fasting, who is in the midst of a crowd and yet alone, who is awake while sleeping, because only such a man attains to liberation while in the world and finds the divine in matter.

Someone has said, "The world should not be in the mind, the mind should not be in the world." This is the key. And if the first half of the maxim is perfected, the second half follows on its own. The first half is the cause; the latter, its effect. If the first is perfected the second is its natural consequence. Those who begin with the second half are mistaken, because that does not work, the second half is not the cause, not the root. So I say the maxim is only this: The world should not be in the mind. The remaining is not part of the maxim, it is the consequence of the maxim. If the world is not in the mind, the mind does not go to the world. That which is not in the mind cannot pull the mind.

In *samadhi*, enlightenment, there is no object to be known, hence the state of *samadhi* cannot be called knowledge. It certainly isn't knowledge in the ordinary sense but at the same time it isn't ignorance either. There is nothing there for not-knowing either. It is different from both knowledge and ignorance. It is neither knowing nor not-knowing of any object, for there is no object at all. There is only subjectivity. There is only that which knows. There is no knowledge of any object there, but only the knowing – consciousness empty of content.

Someone once asked a monk, "What is meditation?" He replied, "To be in that which is near is meditation."

What is near you? Except for your self, isn't everything else at a distance from you? Only you are near your self. But by deserting yourself, you are always somewhere else – you are always somewhere in the neighborhood. But you are not to be in the neighborhood, you are to be in yourself. That is meditation. When you are nowhere and your mind too is nowhere, even then you are somewhere. That being somewhere is meditation.

When you are nowhere, you are in your self. And that is not being in the neighborhood; that is not being away. That is inwardness; that is nearness, intimacy. Only by being there does one awaken into the truth. It is by being in the neighborhood that you have lost everything and it is by being in your self that it all can be regained.

I don't ask you to renounce the world, I ask you to transform yourself. By denying the world you will not change, but when you have changed, the world ceases to be the world for you. True religion is not world-rejecting, it is self-transforming. Don't think of the world but of your outlook in relation to the world. You have to change that. It is because of your outlook that there is the world and there is bondage. It is not the world, but your outlook that is the bondage. Once your outlook is changed, the whole existence changes for you. There is no fault in the world. The fault lies in you and your outlook.

The science for transformation of life is called meditation. Through analysis, physical science reaches the atom and atomic power, but meditation reaches the soul and soul power. Through the former, the mystery hidden in matter is discovered; through the latter, the universe hidden within the self is revealed. But the latter is more important than the former because there is nothing in existence more important than one's own self.

Man has lost his balance because he knows a lot about matter but nothing about himself. He has learned how to dive into the unfathomable depths of the ocean and how to fly into the amazing heights of space but he has completely forgotten how to enter into his own self. This is a suicidal state. This is exactly our misery. Meditation can free you from this imbalance. It needs to be taught. Only through meditation can the birth of a new man in the true sense take place and can the foundations of a new humanity be laid.

Science has declared man's conquest over matter; now man has to conquer himself as well. His conquest of matter has made it imperative that he now know himself and conquer himself. Otherwise, his conquest of the unlimited power of matter will become his own annihilation – because power in the hands of ignorance is always poisonous and suicidal. If science is in the hands of the ignorant, the combination is destructive. But if science is in the hands of the self-knowing, it will lead to the birth of an unprecedented creative energy that can transform this earth into a paradise.

That is why I say that the destiny and the future of man are now in the hands of meditation. Meditation is the science of the future because it is the science of man.

CHAPTER 15

With Infinite Awaiting

What shall I say to you today? We will be departing this evening and I see that your hearts are already heavy at the very thought of that moment. It was only five days ago that we all came here to this lonely place – and who thought of departure then?

But don't forget that going is inevitably inherent in coming. They are two sides of the same coin. Although they can only be seen separately they are simultaneously together. Because of the gap of time between them we become deluded. But anyone who looks a little deeper will find that in meeting itself parting is inherent, that in happiness itself sorrow is inherent and that in birth itself death is inherent. Indeed there is hardly any difference between coming and going – or rather, there is no difference at all. It is the same in life. Hardly have you come, than the process of going has begun. And isn't what we call staying merely a preparation for leaving?

Really, what is the distance between birth and death? The distance between them can become vast, infinite. If your life becomes a spiritual attainment, this distance will become infinite. If your life becomes a spiritual attainment, death will become *moksha*, ultimate liberation. While there is not much distance between birth and death, the distance, the difference between birth and *moksha* is infinite. That distance is as great as the one between body and soul, between a dream and the truth. That distance is the greatest. No two points are further apart.

The illusion that "I am the body" is death; the realization that "I am the soul" is *moksha*, ultimate liberation. And life is an opportunity for the realization of this truth. If this opportunity is used properly and not wasted in vain, the distance between birth and death becomes infinite.

There can be, as well, a great distance between your coming here and your departure – a tremendous distance, in just the few days we have spent here. Isn't it possible that the one who is returning is no more the same as the one who had come? Isn't it possible you may return as an entirely new and transformed person?

If you want it, this revolution or transformation can take place in a single moment. Five days are too many. Otherwise it may not even take place in five life times, what to say of five days? Just one moment of will, of total will, is enough. A whole life without will is nothing.

Remember that will, not time, is the important thing. The achievements of the world happen in time; those of truth, in will. The intensity of will gives a fathomless depth and an infinite expanse to a single moment. As a matter of fact, in the intensity of will, time ceases to exist and only eternity remains.

Will is the door which liberates you from time and unites you with eternity. Let your will deepen and intensify. Let it pervade your every breath. Let it be in your memory, asleep or awake. Only through it can a new birth take place, a birth which knows no death. That alone is real birth.

There is a birth of the physical body that inevitably ends in death. I do not call this real birth. How can something that ends in death be the beginning of life? But there is another birth that does not end in death. It is the real birth, because its culmination is in deathlessness. It is toward this birth that over these few days I have been inviting you and urging you. It is for this birth that we gathered here. But merely coming together here is of no consequence. If each one of you gives birth to a thirst inside and makes a crystallized call, then this determined and integrated state of mind will bring you to the real birth. The truth is always very near, but you need determination, you need will to approach it. The thirst for truth is there in you, but a determined will is equally necessary. Only when it is united with will, does thirst become a spiritual endeavor.

What does "will" mean?

A man once asked a mystic the way to attain God. The mystic looked into his eyes and saw thirst. The mystic was on his way to the river so he asked the man to accompany him and promised to show him the way to attain God after they had bathed.

They arrived at the river, as soon as the man plunged into the water the mystic grabbed the man's head and pushed it down into the water with great force. The man began to struggle to free himself from the mystic's grip. His life was in danger. He was much weaker than the mystic but his latent strength gradually began to stir and soon it became impossible for the mystic to hold him down. The man pushed himself to the limits and was eventually able to surface up. He was shocked. It was almost impossible for him to understand the mystic's strange behavior: Was the mystic mad? And the mystic was laughing loudly as well.

After the man could catch his breath the mystic asked him, "Friend, when you were under the water what desires did you have in your mind?" The man said, "Desires! there weren't desires, there was just one desire – to get a breath of air." The mystic said, "This is the secret of attaining God. This is will. And your will awakened all your latent powers."

It is in such a moment of intense will that great strength is generated, and man transits from the world into the truth. It is through will that the transition from the world into truth and from the dream into truth, takes place.

At this time, at the hour of our parting, I want to remind you of this: will is needed. And what else is needed? A continuity in your spiritual endeavor is needed. Your spiritual effort should have no gaps. Have you ever seen a waterfall coming down from the mountains? It is a constant stream of falling water that eventually breaks the rocks. If you constantly endeavor to break the rocks of ignorance, those very rocks that appeared to be not giving way at all in the beginning, will one day turn into dust and you will find your way.

The path is certainly found, but it is not found ready-made. One has to create it through one's efforts. And what dignity this is for man, how dignified it is that we attain truth by our own efforts.

Mahavira wanted to convey this by his use of the word *shramana* for the seeker. Truth is attained by *shrama*, labor. The truth is not alms given in charity, it is an attainment. You need will, constant effort and infinite awaiting. Truth is infinite, and therefore an infinite awaiting and patience are necessary for it. The divine only descends in endless awaiting. Those who have no patience cannot attain God. In these moments of our parting, I wanted to remind you of this as well.

Finally, I am reminded of a story. Although quite imaginary, it is perfectly true.

An angel passed a spot where an old monk was sitting. The monk said to the angel, "Please ask God how long it will still take for me to attain to liberation." Near the old monk a very young, newly-initiated sannyasin lived under a banyan tree. The angel also asked the young sannyasin if he wanted him to ask God about his liberation as well. But the sannyasin did not say a word. He was quiet, calm and silent.

After some time the angel returned. He said to the old monk, "I asked God about your liberation. He says it will take three more lifetimes."

The old man grew furious and his eyes became bloodshot. He threw away his rosary and said, "Three more lifetimes! It's atrocious!"

Then the angel went to the young man under the banyan tree and said to him, "I also asked God about you. He said you will have to practice your spiritual discipline for as many lifetimes as there are leaves on the banyan tree under which you are sitting."

The young sannyasin's eyes filled with bliss, he jumped up and began to dance saying, "In that case I have attained! There are so many trees on the earth and so many leaves on each of them! If I will attain to the divine in only as many births as there are leaves on this small banyan tree, then I have already attained right now."

This is the milieu in which one reaps the harvest of truth. And do you know the end of this story? The young sannyasin kept on dancing and dancing and in that dance itself, that very moment he became liberated, he attained to the divine. That moment of tranquility and of infinite love and awaiting was everything. Such a moment itself *is* the liberation. This I call infinite awaiting. And he who has infinite awaiting attains everything here and now. This state of being is itself that attainment.

Are you ready for such an awaiting? With this question I bid you farewell. May existence give you strength that the river of your life reaches the ocean of truth. This is my wish and my prayer.

ABOUT OSHO

Osho's unique contribution to the understanding of who we are defies categorization. Mystic and scientist, a rebellious spirit whose sole interest is to alert humanity to the urgent need to discover a new way of living. To continue as before is to invite threats to our very survival on this unique and beautiful planet.

His essential point is that only by changing ourselves, one individual at a time, can the outcome of all our "selves" – our societies, our cultures, our beliefs, our world – also change. The doorway to that change is meditation.

Osho the scientist has experimented and scrutinized all the approaches of the past and examined their effects on the modern human being and responded to their shortcomings by creating a new starting point for the hyperactive 21st Century mind: OSHO Active Meditations.

Once the agitation of a modern lifetime has started to settle, "activity" can melt into "passivity," a key starting point of real meditation. To support this next step, Osho has transformed the ancient "art of listening" into a subtle contemporary methodology: the OSHO Talks. Here words become music, the listener discovers who is listening, and the awareness moves from what is being heard to the individual doing the listening. Magically, as silence arises, what needs to be heard is understood directly, free from the distraction of a mind that can only interrupt and interfere with this delicate process.

These thousands of talks cover everything from the individual quest for meaning to the most urgent social and political issues facing society today. Osho's books are not written but are transcribed from audio and video recordings of these extemporaneous talks to international audiences. As he puts it, "So remember: whatever I am saying is not just for you...I am talking also for the future generations."

Osho has been described by *The Sunday Times* in London as one of the "1000 Makers of the 20th Century" and by American author Tom Robbins as "the most dangerous man since Jesus Christ." *Sunday Mid-Day* (India) has selected Osho as one of ten people – along with Gandhi, Nehru and Buddha – who have changed the destiny of India.

About his own work Osho has said that he is helping to create the conditions for the birth of a new kind of human being. He often characterizes this new human being as "Zorba the Buddha" – capable both of enjoying the earthy pleasures of a Zorba the Greek and the silent serenity of a Gautama the Buddha.

Running like a thread through all aspects of Osho's talks and meditations is a vision that encompasses both the timeless wisdom of all ages past and the highest potential of today's (and tomorrow's) science and technology.

Osho is known for his revolutionary contribution to the science of inner transformation, with an approach to meditation that acknowledges the accelerated pace of contemporary life. His unique OSHO Active Meditations™ are designed to first release the accumulated stresses of body and mind, so that it is then easier to take an experience of stillness and thought-free relaxation into daily life.

Two autobiographical works by the author are available:

Autobiography of a Spiritually Incorrect Mystic,
St Martins Press, New York (book and eBook)

Glimpses of a Golden Childhood,
OSHO Media International, Pune, India (book and eBook)

OSHO INTERNATIONAL
MEDITATION RESORT

Each year the Meditation Resort welcomes thousands of people from more than 100 countries. The unique campus provides an opportunity for a direct personal experience of a new way of living – with more awareness, relaxation, celebration and creativity. A great variety of around-the-clock and around-the-year program options are available. Doing nothing and just relaxing is one of them!

All of the programs are based on Osho's vision of "Zorba the Buddha" – a qualitatively new kind of human being who is able *both* to participate creatively in everyday life *and* to relax into silence and meditation.

Location
Located 100 miles southeast of Mumbai in the thriving modern city of Pune, India, the OSHO International Meditation Resort is a holiday destination with a difference. The Meditation Resort is spread over 28 acres of spectacular gardens in a beautiful tree-lined residential area.

OSHO Meditations

A full daily schedule of meditations for every type of person includes both traditional and revolutionary methods, and particularly the OSHO Active Meditations™. The daily meditation program takes place in what must be the world's largest meditation hall, the OSHO Auditorium.

OSHO Multiversity

Individual sessions, courses and workshops cover everything from creative arts to holistic health, personal transformation, relationship and life transition, transforming meditation into a lifestyle for life and work, esoteric sciences, and the "Zen" approach to sports and recreation. The secret of the OSHO Multiversity's success lies in the fact that all its programs are combined with meditation, supporting the understanding that as human beings we are far more than the sum of our parts.

OSHO Basho Spa

The luxurious Basho Spa provides for leisurely open-air swimming surrounded by trees and tropical green. The uniquely styled, spacious Jacuzzi, the saunas, gym, tennis courts...all these are enhanced by their stunningly beautiful setting.

Cuisine

A variety of different eating areas serve delicious Western, Asian and Indian vegetarian food – most of it organically grown especially for the Meditation Resort. Breads and cakes are baked in the resort's own bakery.

Night life

There are many evening events to choose from – dancing being at the top of the list! Other activities include full-moon meditations beneath the stars, variety shows, music performances and meditations for daily life.

Facilities

You can buy all of your basic necessities and toiletries in the Galleria. The Multimedia Gallery sells a large range of OSHO media products. There is also a bank, a travel agency and a Cyber Café on-campus. For those who enjoy shopping, Pune provides all the options, ranging from traditional and ethnic Indian products to all of the global brand-name stores.

Accommodation

You can choose to stay in the elegant rooms of the OSHO Guesthouse, or for longer stays on campus you can select one of the OSHO Living-In programs. Additionally there is a plentiful variety of nearby hotels and serviced apartments.

www.osho.com/meditationresort
www.osho.com/guesthouse
www.osho.com/livingin

MORE OSHO BOOKS

The God Conspiracy:
The Path from Superstition to Super Consciousness

Discover the Buddha: 53 Meditations to Meet the Buddha Within
Gold Nuggets: Messages from Existence

OSHO Classics
The Book of Wisdom: The Heart of Tibetan Buddhism.
The Mustard Seed: The Revolutionary Teachings of Jesus
Ancient Music in the Pines: In Zen, Mind Suddenly Stops
The Empty Boat: Encounters with Nothingness
A Bird on the Wing: Zen Anecdotes for Everyday Life
The Path of Yoga: Discovering the Essence and Origin of Yoga
And the Flowers Showered: The Freudian Couch and Zen
Nirvana: The Last Nightmare: Learning to Trust in Life
The Goose Is Out: Zen in Action
Absolute Tao: Subtle Is the Way to Love, Happiness and Truth
The Tantra Experience: Evolution through Love
Tantric Transformation: When Love Meets Meditation

Pillars of Consciousness (illustrated)
BUDDHA: His Life and Teachings and Impact on Humanity
ZEN: Its History and Teachings and Impact on Humanity
TANTRA: The Way of Acceptance
TAO: The State and the Art

Authentic Living

Danger: Truth at Work: The Courage to Accept the Unknowable
The Magic of Self-Respect: Awakening to Your Own Awareness
Born With a Question Mark in Your Heart

OSHO eBooks and "OSHO-Singles"

Emotions: Freedom from Anger, Jealousy and Fear
Meditation: The First and Last Freedom
What Is Meditation?
The Book of Secrets: 112 Meditations to Discover the Mystery Within

20 Difficult Things to Accomplish in This World
Compassion, Love and Sex
Hypnosis in the Service of Meditation
Why Is Communication So Difficult, Particularly between Lovers?
Bringing Up Children
Why Should I Grieve Now?: facing a loss and letting it go
Love and Hate: ust two sides of the same coin

Next Time You Feel Angry...
Next Time You Feel Lonely...
Next Time You Feel Suicidal…

OSHO Media BLOG
http://oshomedia.blog.osho.com

FOR MORE INFORMATION

www. **OSHO** .com

a comprehensive multi-language website including a magazine,
OSHO Books, OSHO Talks in audio and video formats, the
OSHO Library text archive in English and Hindi and extensive
information about OSHO Meditations. You will also find the
program schedule of the OSHO Multiversity and information
about the OSHO International Meditation Resort.

http://OSHO.com/AllAboutOSHO
http://OSHO.com/Resort
http://OSHO.com/Shop
http://www.youtube.com/OSHO
http://www.Twitter.com/OSHO
http://www.facebook.com/pages/OSHO.International

To contact OSHO International Foundation:
www.osho.com/oshointernational,
oshointernational@oshointernational.com